IMPERFECTLY

HOLY

Holiness is a Process

R.C. Blakes, Jr.

IMPERFECTLY HOLY

PUBLISHED BY

UNTAPPED POTENTIAL
PUBLISHING

P.O. BOX 84355
PEARLAND, TX 77584

www.untappedpotentialpublishing.com

DEDICATION

This book is dedicated to the present generation and to those coming behind me. This is dedicated to every person that has a desire to live a Christ-like life but has not had any real instruction. This is for the young person who has a vibrant love for God, but is trying to reconcile the social and biological temptations of youth, with the constant reality of biblical values. This book is also for the mature Christian who has struggled with a private vice for many years with a corresponding shame. This book is written for the person who is simply seeking to approach a relationship with Christ in a sincere and dedicated fashion. It is for one that desires a faith that is not only pronounced but demonstrated. I dedicate this book to you. You are me and I am you.

Holiness is not an impossible ideal. It is not just some religious standard without a realistic life application process. I've been there. I have felt the guilt and the shame that comes from loving God, wanting to please Him, and falling short.

This book is dedicated to you. I hope that my many years of experience (both good and bad) may amount to an impartation of wisdom that will change your life. Holiness is not perfection—it's transformation.

My prayer is that this book and its content will begin to renew your mind and transform your thinking to live freely for God.

CONTENTS

INTRODUCTION

MY STORY

I am the namesake and eldest son of a most iconic and respected religious figure (Bishop Robert Blakes, Sr.). His voice resonated throughout America at the latter end of the 20th century and into the 21st century. His message was one of power and a call to holiness.

I was his son but my life certainly did not model his message. I was an unwed father at just fifteen years of age. I had been sexually active long before then. I was a womanizer, a liar, and a cheat. I got married and divorced, and was never faithful to any woman.

On top of all of this, I was always in the church. My life reminds me of the sons of Eli who desecrated the House of God with their sexual indiscretions. I was in the church and listening to the messages of sanctification and holiness but could never reconcile my life with God's standard. I started out pretending that I was perfect but I was actually growing worse in private.

I eventually was called into ministry. I couldn't believe that God had called me. I DID NOT EVEN WANT

TO PREACH! Why me?

As time went on, I grew weary of preaching one thing and living something else. I didn't think it was possible for me to change. From what I had been hearing from church folk, I should have become perfect overnight. *I MUST HAVE BEEN DEFECTIVE.* I eventually learned that most of the saints were acting. Most of us were preaching one thing and living something else. However, being a hypocrite didn't sit well with me. I was troubled by the inconsistencies in my character. Was I even saved? It grieved me but I did not know what to do about it.

To make a long story short, one day the Holy Spirit arrested me and began to teach me how to overcome the temptations and weaknesses of my flesh. **I began to learn that my sanctification would never be an instantaneous perfection but a life-long process of transformation.** I learned that holiness is not perfection as in flawless perfection; holiness is perfection as in a constant spiritual maturation.

Every day I am growing and becoming more and more like Christ. I am not perfect; I am perfecting. Many days I become impatient with myself but the fact remains that holiness is a process. I have a perfect heart that is expressing itself a little more each day upon the canvas of my life.

Today I am a faithful husband and a respected voice in the Body of Christ. I am so very far from where I once was; God has done marvelous things in my life. With all of this, I am still in the process. I am still not perfect. I am not in any position to judge anyone else. I AM IMPERFECTLY HOLY.

IT'S A PROCESS

I have a very bad habit of buying things that require assembling and then bypassing the manufacturer's assembly instructions. I usually attempt to go directly to the finished product without the required process. I love shortcuts! Rather than read the instructions, I usually try to put an item together based on the picture on the front of the box. I suppose this most unproductive tendency stems from my childhood love for jigsaw puzzles. As I recall, the puzzle was primarily assembled from the picture on the box. There were no piece-by-piece instructions. For me, this has grown into a generally hurried approach to anything requiring assemblage.

Because of this bad habit, assembling items without referring to the included instructions usually leaves me with a fragile and less-than-stable finished product. This way of thinking can tend to dominate a person's entire life. One might attempt to rush important things that demand time and sequence.

However, my proclivity toward rushed assembly is trivial and of no real consequence when it comes to furniture or toys, but there is a real consequence when it comes to spirituality. The unfortunate fact is that many Christians approach the things of God without ever engaging or understanding that certain spiritual goals and disciplines must be processed into our lives. One such discipline is holiness. Something as blatantly opposite to the base human experience as holiness does not drop out of the sky. **Holiness is a definite process. Holiness is not an instant deposit that transforms a person's nature immediately.** It is a definite discipline that requires a specific process to produce.

The church, in large, tells people to be holy without ever presenting the instruction manual (The Bible). We often leave sincere spiritual babes under the assumption they can attain holy living by positive thinking, following a list of denominational rules, or mimicking the behavior of others. To present the doctrine of holiness as if it is this simple is a blatant misrepresentation of truth and it is irresponsible religious rhetoric.

Many Times, People Who Demand Holiness
of Others Are Rarely Sound in Their Own
Personal Character.

Because of the hypocrisy of many, including those in church leadership, holiness is believed to be unattainable. The common mentality in the religious world is that we should all keep face for the religious crowd, in public, while we fail in private. This way of thinking is not because believers, in general, don't have a desire to live the life God requires; it is because most lack sufficient instruction concerning the process of holy living. When one lacks sufficient knowledge of the process, he ends up in one of two positions; he will either start out with a great zeal to live the perfect life and soon falter in disappointment, or he will view holiness as an impossible demand, and not even try. For instance, the word of God says, *"For I bear them record that they have a zeal of God, but not according to knowledge."* ROMANS 10:2

Zeal is an enthusiastic ambition to do something. Many sincere believers have approached the subject of holiness with an excitement and fervor to live just as Jesus did. A problem arises with the realization that holy living cannot be attained on zeal alone. Many passionate men have fallen under the pressure of attempting to live the sanctified life. The Apostle Paul describes his experience with the struggle of holy living in the book of Romans. He states that *"the things I want to do, I don't do, and the things I don't want to do, those things I do."* ROMANS 7:15

Wanting to live a holy life is not enough. If it were, all genuine believers would never miss the mark, whereas a born-again person has a genuine desire to please God.

I was once such a person. I had a real desire in my heart to please God but could never reconcile the desires of my heart with the actions of my life. I sincerely believed that I should have been perfectly pure and free from all defilement when I was saved. When I messed up, I felt filthy and worthless. It took weeks for me to shake off the powerful sense of guilt I felt.

The greatest disservice this false religious assumption inflicted upon me was that I began to doubt the genuineness of my salvation. Have you ever thought this way? Here's how my thought process went: If I am really saved, why do I have such a problem with womanizing? How could I have been born into the home of a prominent preacher and possess these private struggles? How could I have had a child out of wedlock? The thing that confused me most was that I never heard people in church talk about having these kinds of temptations and weaknesses. Everybody I met was hitting the mark, at least according to them. I concluded that something was severely wrong with me.

For the longest time, I was bound to this false idea that I should have automatically been just like Jesus if I really had been saved on that faithful Sunday morning. Then, out of nowhere, I read the Bible. WOW! I never thought to read the Bible for myself. The Bible was just a decoration for the podium at church and for the coffee table at home. As I began to read the Word, I came upon some interesting passages that shed a little light into the darkness of my confusion. Passages like ROMANS 12:2, which says: *"And be not conformed to this world, but be ye transformed by the renewing of your mind."*

There are two words that stand out in this passage; *transformed* and *renewing*. The suffixes used at the end of each word, and the way the words are used in the text, clearly point out something important: We are transformed by some sequential process and not an instantaneous spiritual phenomenon. In clearer terms, we must embrace a particular spiritual process if we are to be transformed.

There is another passage that caught my attention as I read the Bible for myself. It is found in 2 CORINTHIANS 3:18 and states, *"But we all, with open face beholding as in a glass the glory of the Lord, are changed into the same image from GLORY TO GLORY, even as by the Spirit of the Lord."*

The phrase that captured my attention and began to set me free from the bondage of ignorance was the phrase *"glory to glory."* This phrase identifies for us that our being changed into the image of Christ will happen on different levels.

> Christ-Likeness Is Not a Simple Destination, It Is a Lifelong Journey. We Must Evolve into His Likeness.

After toiling with this issue for many years, it finally hit home that living the life of holiness is a process. The trick of the enemy is to make us feel as if holiness should be attained overnight; consequently, when it does not happen automatically, he destroys us with guilt. I've been there and done that, but never again!

I write this book not as one who has fully arrived, but I've made some serious progress. What I can rejoice in is that I have learned the principles to operate within the will of God. It has freed me to grow into the image and likeness of Christ. As much as I love shortcuts, there are no shortcuts to living a life that is committed to God. The Apostle Paul stated it this way: *"I die daily."* Holiness is God's will, and is possible to attain once you learn the process.

SECTION A

WHAT IS HOLINESS, REALLY?

CHAPTER 1

MISCONCEPTIONS ABOUT HOLINESS

Trying to narrow down a definition of holiness today is like searching for a cold cereal in a grocery store. There are so many colors and types; you can spend the day gazing at the wall of brands and never make a decision, or end up totally displeased with the brand you settled on.

The Concept of Holiness Has Been so Misconstrued That It Has Become One of the Most Confusing Subjects.

It was an uncertain time in the United States of America, and the entire world was glued to television screens, radios, and newspapers. All wanted to hear what President Bill Clinton, the forty-second president of the United States of America, had to say in his own defense as he fought against accusations of sexual misconduct in the White House. President Clinton, who is arguably one of the greatest political minds of all time, a scholar, statesman, orator, educator, and author, confused the entire world with his definition of a simple little term. I won't elaborate on the specific terminology he twisted into knots to finesse his way out of hot water, but when

President Clinton finished with his muddling of such a simple term, no one understood it. That incident reminds me of the million-and-one definitions of holiness that religious people have adopted. Some of us have been in the church for years and still don't have a solid or workable definition of holiness. We are still confused. We respond affirmatively to the concept while having no grasp of the principle.

It Is Very Important That We Gain a Clear and Viable Definition of Holiness.

There's a drove of opinions concerning this matter. In certain religious sects, the concept of holiness is diminished to something as meaningless as a mere dress code. The antiquated sentiment of this group is that long dresses and dark clothing are equivalent to being holy. Other groups have limited holiness to their particular religious' persuasion. In these settings, to be holy requires having one's membership with a certain organization.

As a kid, I was blessed to spend some time in the company of the late Bishop G. E. Patterson, Presiding Bishop of the Church of God in Christ. One day he said, *"Jesus never died for an organization, he died for a living organism."*

Joining an institution does not impact your personal moral constitution. Some of the least holy people on the planet have been members of religious organizations all of their lives. In fact, most of the blood spilled around the world is in the name of religion and piety.

We may all have our individual beliefs about holiness; nonetheless, it means nothing if God is retaining a different position. Our religious organizations may indoctrinate us to accept their view, but if God has another, what's the use? After all, it starts and finishes with Him, not the preachers, authors, theologians, or self-righteous church members. Our aim must always be to live in accordance with God's word. I am done with following these empty man-made concepts. I need to do it God's way!

One of the Terms Used for Holiness in the Greek New Testament Signifies Something Being Set Apart to God, or Something for God's Use.

The author of the book of Romans says, "*I speak after the manner of men because of the infirmity of your flesh: for as ye have yielded your members servants to uncleanness and to iniquity unto iniquity; even so now yield your members servants to righteousness unto holiness.*" ROMANS 6:19

The Greek term *hagiasmos* is used in this text for holiness. It speaks of the conduct that should accompany those who have been born again by the blood of Christ. Notice that the writer uses the term *yield*. **The basis of holiness is to yield one's life to the purposes and plan of God, as we come out of the world.**

The Action of Holy Living Is Characterized by Separation. If You're Not Willing to Separate from the World, You'll Never Walk in the True Virtue of Holiness.

The word of God declares in 2 CORINTHIANS 6:17: *"Wherefore come out from among them, and be ye separate, saith the Lord, and touch not the unclean thing; and I will receive you."* This is an admonishment to come out from among the world (the culture and philosophies of the secular society). **We can't remain entangled and overly involved with worldly ideals and pursue a life of holiness.** We must begin to establish ourselves in a place that we strictly reserve for God's purposes.

Holiness Is Living a Separated Lifestyle. It's the Honor of Reserving and Preserving One's Life for God's Use Only.

When I was a kid, my mother would put my dad's food on a special plate. Her instructions were, *do not touch your dad's plate.* I knew not to ever put my hands on that plate because it had been set aside. In biblical terms, my dad's plate was *sanctified*. It was set apart. It was not for my use. It was off limits. This is a wonderful glimpse into the legitimate holiness experience. Holiness transcends rituals or religion, **holiness is about being personally and sincerely set apart to God, and making yourself off limits to the world.**

HOLINESS IS NOT PERFECTION

Another false conception of holiness is that it means to be perfect. I am the first to admit that the process of holiness is demanding, and it will involve every fiber of your physical, spiritual, and emotional being to activate. However, perfection, in the sense of flawlessness or faultlessness, is not a requirement.

If Flawlessness Were a Requirement of Holiness, None of Us Would Need to Even Try.

There's an interesting definition I found in the *American Dictionary of the English Language*. The dictionary states this: *holiness is purity of heart or dispositions; sanctified affections; piety; moral goodness, but not perfect.* Notice the dictionary makes it clear that holiness is a laundry list of excellent qualities but does not include perfection.

Many People Don't Even Attempt to Reach for the
Holiness Lifestyle Because They Start Out with the
Spurious Notion That Holiness is Equivalent to
Unblemished Perfection.

The Bible does challenge us to *be perfect*, but it is
not speaking of faultless perfection. The perfection of the
Bible is usually in reference to maturity or the process of
growing into spiritual things. For instance, MATTHEW
5:48 says: *"Be ye therefore perfect, even as your Father
which is in heaven is perfect."*

At first glance, this text appears to call for flawless
perfection, but when we look a bit deeper, we see the
real meaning of the text. The word *perfect* is the Greek
word *teleios* and it means *to be of full age.* The text is
referencing maturity or being complete, not perfection.
ONLY GOD IS PERFECT.

WHAT HOLINESS IS NOT

In Some Strange Sense, Our Best Way to Understand
What Holiness Really Is, Is to Understand What It's Not.

There is another common misrepresentation of
biblical holiness. It's called conformity. Consider the
biblical passage that states: *"And be not **conformed** to this
world: but be ye transformed by the renewing of your*

mind, that ye may prove what is that good, and acceptable, and perfect, will of God." ROMANS 12:2

Most people, when reading this text, immediately associate the term *conformed* to the obvious illicit activities of the "world." In other words, we may conclude that it means to not conform to nightclubs, liberal sexuality, or any blatant immorality. We assume it's speaking of things that are far removed from religion. To have this particular view certainly is not wrong but it is narrow, limited, and deceptive. The word *conformed* is the Greek term *suschematizo*. It means *to fashion alike, conform to the same pattern (figuratively): to fashion according to*. Notice how the definitions of *conformed* all point to an external adherence to something. It has nothing to do with anything internal. It's all about shaping the outside to model an image.

Another angle on this text for your consideration might be to think about the potential of religious conformity. All conformity is not necessarily divorced from the sacred ranks. I have been in the church environment all of my life and can testify that we have people who sit in churches every Sunday and simply take on the likeness of what they see around them, and never experience a real genuine internal transformation.

Because We Have Not Understood the Real Process of Holiness, Most of Us Have Settled for Decorating the Outside While Never Dealing with the Inside.

This amounts to nothing more than religious conformity. One day, Jesus judged a certain group of religious people and said, *"Woe unto you, scribes and Pharisees, hypocrites! for ye make clean the outside of the cup and of the platter, but within they are full of extortion and excess. Thou blind Pharisee, cleanse first that which is within the cup and platter, that the outside of them may be clean also."* MATTHEW 23:25–26

Jesus was speaking to the scribes and Pharisees. These were the most religious men of that day. He talks about how they are content with cleaning the outside, while the inside remained defiled. This is what's happening in the church today.

We Are Dressing Like It and Talking Like It, But Few Are Realizing It. We Are Cleaning the Outside of the Cup and the Inside Is Untouched.

Jesus also called them hypocrites. Don't get nervous. I am in no position to criticize or condemn anyone. Condemnation is not the purpose of this document. In fact, my view on hypocrisy is a little different than most people. *A hypocrite is simply an actor or one that puts on a performance.* When we look at the word from that broad angle, we have more hypocrites in the church than we care to acknowledge. I believe that there are sincere hypocrites as well as plain ungodly classical hypocrites.

It is clear that there are varying degrees of hypocrisy. Think about it. How many people are sitting in our church pews who don't have a clue as to what to do to live holy, and have simply settled for religious conformity or acting like the crowd? They may have a true desire but lack an understanding of how to accomplish it. I consider this sincere hypocrisy. The only reason they act is because they have not identified a pragmatic process to aid them in achieving their real desire for holiness. They are not willfully deceiving; they are merely surviving.

The author of Romans also used the word *transformed.* One passage says: *"don't be conformed but be transformed."* ROMANS 12:2

This word carries a different meaning than the word *conformed.* The term conformed refers to an external alteration of the façade (the superficial face). *Transformed* means something totally different.

To Be Transformed Means to Change from the Inside to the Outside. It Means to Evolve Into Something Totally New and Different.

The text says: *"be transformed by the renewing of your mind."* When it mentions the mind, it lets us know that it's an internal experience. **Transformation is a real process that happens from the inside of the heart and reveals its effects in the lifestyle.** It goes on to express that once we are truly transformed, we will *"prove the acceptable and perfect will of God."* This simply means that when something actually changes on the inside it will automatically show up on the outside.

God Is Not Accepting Religious Conformation; He Wants the Transformation of Your Heart and Mind.

With all of this said, let's get down to the heart of the matter. **What is holiness?** If it is not flawless perfection, not religious conformity, and not the result of some denominational affiliation, **what is it?**

Holiness Defined: Holiness Is the Daily and Lifelong Process of a Believer, Willingly Obeying God and Transforming into the Image of Christ.

From this very practical definition we see that holiness is not some instantaneous arrival at moral perfection. It is a lifelong journey and process.

We Become Holy from One Degree to the Next.

The main point in this definition is that it is something that we must willingly submit to. God does not constrain us or force holiness upon us. It is only acceptable to Him when we willingly and purposefully consecrate our lives to Him by obeying His word.

SUMMARY OF CHAPTER ONE

1. Holiness has nothing to do with perfection.
2. Conforming to religious rules is not holiness.
3. When people don't understand how to attain the holiness lifestyle, they will settle for acting rather than genuine transformation.
4. Holiness is a lifelong process of transforming into the image of Christ.
5. Holiness is the act of obeying God on purpose.

CHAPTER 2

FACTS ABOUT HOLINESS

Somewhere at about ten years of age, I learned a very specific style of communication. I would employ this particular communication style when I didn't want to face the real facts of a particular matter. For instance, I used it on teachers when they would ask, "Where is your homework, Robert?" I used it on my mother if she asked why the dishes were not washed. This style of communication involved beating around the bush and dealing with other issues to avoid the facts. I thought that I had mastered it until I tried it on my dad. He would interrogate me, and when I would attempt to elude the real facts he would always forcefully bring me back to the issue. He would say something like, "Bob, nothing but the facts!"

When we learn the facts, we can come to an understanding of the truth. Just like Dad forced me to get straight to the point and to expose the bare facts, we too must get down to where the rubber meets the road concerning holiness. There are some very real and necessary details that every believer must understand to have an opportunity to succeed at living the holiness lifestyle. The Word of God states that God is holy and requires the same of His people. The Bible is filled with numerous commands directed to God's people to live holy.

Since this is the case, why is it that most of the Body of Christ ignores the very subject of holiness? We don't hear it preached or taught much in most churches. Rarely can we tune into Christian television and hear a complete message on holiness. I haven't seen much of it mentioned on social media platforms. Why? Is it that we have become so defiled that we don't care anymore? I think not. Maybe it's because few Christians really understand the facts of holiness. It is our tendency to avoid the things we don't understand. We, in our own human limitations, often read into the subject rather than seek to understand what God's word is actually communicating. Leadership has failed the Body of Christ in this area.

We Have Preached Holiness but We've
Failed to Teach It.

To preach it without teaching it is the same as shouting "fire, the house is burning down!" and not to provide directives for escape. The only way to truly empower people is to teach them. Wherever there is a deficiency in the lives of God's people, the blame starts with the condition of that people's leadership.

2 CHRONICLES 15:3 says: *"Now for a long season Israel hath been without the true God, and without a teaching priest, and without law."*

FACT NUMBER ONE ABOUT HOLINESS:
The Quality of Your Spiritual Leader Will Influence Your Lifestyle.

The quality of any people is directly linked to their spiritual guidance. Think about it; in a church where the pastor is tolerant of immorality, at least that level of immorality abounds in that congregation. If the pastor has a certain moral flaw or weakness, it is magnified in the moral fiber of that congregation.

On the other hand, if a pastor is a godly and sincere individual, the same magnifies itself in the flock. One of the most important relationships in any Christian's life is the pastor relationship.

The Quality of Your Spiritual Leadership Is the Forecast of Your Future.

If you are going to elevate your lifestyle to the standard of God, you must be exposed to the living Word of God. The Word must be presented in a fashion that is life applicable. The men and women of God we submit to must have more on their agendas than worthless emotional sessions or dead religious formality. As a member of spiritual leadership in the Body of Christ, I believe that one of the greatest sins of modern clergy is that we have not equipped the people to maximize their real potential in God. Consequently, God is raising men and women that will minister with ethics, passion, and transparency without compromise.

I remember when my life began to transform. My pastor, Bishop Robert Blakes Sr., had been in-filled with the power of the Holy Spirit and started to live the Spirit-controlled life. Prior to this experience he had been a conformist Baptist preacher his entire ministry. Needless to say, his ministry took on a total different character after his experience. He went from ritualism to relationship. His preaching ministry went from merely passing over the text on Sundays with little to no life-altering effect, to suddenly unfolding the deep mysteries of the scripture. There was an unusual authority accompanying his words; they began to sink into my heart and create life.

In JOHN 6:63 Jesus says: *"The words that I speak unto you, they are spirit, and they are life."*

In this text, Jesus says, His words produce life. That is exactly what began to happen to me under my pastor's ministry. His words began to bring life to me.

In the beginning I did not appreciate this unusual deposit of truth that was being made into my heart, but it started to effect change in my thinking and life. When the quality of my spiritual leader elevated, my life was changed.

The Very First Issue You Must Address Is the Level of the Person You Call Your Spiritual Leader.

This is a day when spiritual discernment and discretion are mandatory. You will never go beyond the person you follow intently.

FACT NUMBER TWO ABOUT HOLINESS: Holiness Is Our Gift to God.

The psalmist asked the question, *"What shall I render unto the LORD for all his benefits toward me"?* PSALM 116:12

The psalmist is contemplating what to give God to express his gratitude for all of God's benefits. We like to think that the financial offerings we give are sufficient to express our appreciation to God. The reality is that our offerings are just a response of obedience to God for allowing us to be stewards of His resources.

The Real Offering Is the Presentation of Our Lives on the Altar of Sanctification.

It is when we say "no" to our way and "yes" to His way that we begin to develop a momentum towards pleasing Him. *We must get beyond the idea that holy living is merely a restraint and understand it is our truest gift to God.* The Father gave His son that we might have eternal life and our gift to Him is the surrendering of our lives to His will. We don't live holy to be saved; we live holy because we are saved, and we understand the great price that was paid for our salvation. God's son died in my place for my sins. If Jesus can die for me, the least I can do is live for Him.

Holiness is Our Gift to God for Salvation.

Today's church is overwhelmed with what God can do for us. We want the prosperity of God, we want the healing touch of God, but few are focused on what we can do for God. We want His benefits without offering ourselves. The greatest benefit we may ever receive from the Father is redemption from the penalty of sin. When a person has a genuine realization of being saved from his sins, by no works of his own, it will generate a desire to live for Christ.

The word of God puts it this way: *"For by grace are ye saved through faith; and that not of yourselves: it is the gift of God: Not of works, lest any man should boast. For we are his workmanship, created in Christ Jesus unto good works, which God hath before ordained that we should walk in them."* EPHESIANS 2:8–10

When the writer says we were created unto good works, he is referencing our salvation experience. In other words, we were saved to do good works. You are not saved because of your good works but, when you are truly saved, it will lead you to good works. Holy living is the least we can offer God for the gift of salvation.

The writer of Romans most eloquently puts it this way, *"I beseech you therefore, brethren, by the mercies of God, that ye present your bodies a living sacrifice, holy, acceptable unto God, which is your reasonable service."* ROMANS 12:1

Holiness is very important, even though we hear very little taught of it. It is important to God because it demonstrates our appreciation for His sacrifice. It models His nature to the world and it makes our fellowship with Him possible. Holiness is important to us because it opens the door for us to experience the abundant life that Christ promised us.

As important as holiness is to God and man, religion has served to terribly confuse the issue. We have turned holiness into a complicated list of rules that must be followed to make it to Heaven. Because we have not fully understood holiness, we have not mastered it as a reality in our lives.

A Lack of Understanding Is the Greatest
Hindrance to Holy Living.

FACT NUMBER THREE ABOUT HOLINESS:
Righteousness and Holiness Are Not the Same Thing.

We must understand the difference between righteousness and holiness. Understanding righteousness and how it differs from holiness provides a foundation for building on.

If You Never Get an Understanding of Righteousness,
You'll Never Be Set Free to Live Holy.

Usually in the typical church fellowship, people use the term righteousness to describe or define holiness. This is unfortunate because your righteousness comes before holiness; they are not one and the same.

Righteousness Defined: To Be Called or Declared to Be in
Right Standing by a Ruling Authority.

This truth can be understood by simply observing the workings of a judge's courtroom. If a person is accused of certain crimes and comes before the judge, the decision is sometimes solely up to the judge. It does not matter if the person is guilty or innocent; if the judge calls the person "not guilty," that individual leaves the courtroom acquitted. This is exactly what Christ did for us. Because of Jesus' suffering, the Father judged us as not guilty. We are declared righteous because of Christ and his love.

Righteousness Is a Gift.

Righteousness is simply a gift from God. This truth was one of the most difficult concepts for me to grasp. How could I be so obviously guilty and have God declare me righteous? It has been the experience of being a father myself that has helped me to understand God's position in this matter.

There have been occasions while raising my kids when I would play certain games with them. Sometimes they would be losing and I would declare them winners because I felt like it. In those situations I was sovereign and in total control. There was no authority to overturn my decision to call my children winners. Take a look at what the Bible says in the book of Romans. It says: *"But now the righteousness of God without the law is manifested, being witnessed by the law and the prophets; Even the righteousness of God which is by faith of Jesus Christ unto all and upon all them that believe: for there is no difference: For all have sinned and come short of the glory of God; Being justified freely by his grace through the redemption that is in Christ Jesus."* ROMANS 3:21–22

Notice the text says that God's righteousness is without the law. In other words, it does not come because we follow the rules. The text then lets us know that this righteousness is by faith in Jesus Christ unto all that believe. The text goes further to explain that it is all a product of God's grace, or His unmerited favor bestowed upon those that will simply believe.

Righteousness Is Not Based on What You Do or Don't Do. Righteousness Is Not Performance-Based.

The book of Isaiah makes it very clear that righteousness has nothing to do with works. It says: *"But we are all as an unclean thing, and all our righteousness is as filthy rags; and we all do fade as a leaf; and our iniquities, like the wind, have taken us away."* ISAIAH 64:6

This text uses a very specific phrase: *"our righteousness."* The implication is that there is a counterfeit or man-made righteousness. This is also known as a religious righteousness or self-righteousness. This is the kind of righteousness that struggles to keep rules and rituals as an attempt to please God. The problem with this righteousness is that it will never please God. There is nothing you and I can do, or not do, that would be good enough to satisfy The Holy God.

There's a funny story of a young boy whose mother would leave him at home when she went to work. She said to him, "Don't say anything to anyone while I'm gone, and keep your mouth closed so that people don't know how dumb you are. Keep your mouth closed, do you understand?" The boy said, "Yes, Mama."

While she was out, a co-worker of his mother's came by and asked the young boy if his mother was home. The young boy simply gazed without saying a word. The lady asked if something was wrong with him and he continued to stare. The lady finally got disgusted and said to the boy, "Son, when people ask you questions, learn to speak and don't act so dumb!" Finally the young man's mother returned home and asked if anyone had come by, and did he say anything stupid. The boy said, "Yes, your co-worker came by and I didn't say a word, but she still knew I was dumb anyway."

If this boy talked, he was messed up, and if he stayed quiet, he was doomed. Just like this child couldn't satisfy the demands of his mother or her co-worker, a believer will never be able to do enough, or not enough, to earn righteousness. This is why the Word says *"And that ye put on the new man, which after God is created in righteousness and true holiness. Wherefore putting away lying, speak every man truth with his neighbor: for we are members one of another. Be ye angry, and sin not: let not the sun go down upon your wrath: Neither give place to the devil."* EPHESIANS 4:24–27

Notice how the text makes a distinction between righteousness and holiness. The writer goes as far as to use an interesting phrase; he says: "true holiness." Based on this text, I think it is safe to conclude that there is a false sense of holiness.

I Believe That Most of the Body of Christ Today Is Operating in a False Sense of Holiness.

After a person makes the distinction between righteousness and holiness, he then proceeds to list things that need to be put away. The putting-away process does not take place before righteousness or in conjunction with righteousness; rather, it happens subsequent to or after one has been declared righteous. **Holiness comes after salvation.** Holiness is the daily lifelong process of a believer to willingly obey God and transform into the image of Christ. **Righteousness is imputed at the moment of salvation, then the cleansing of holiness happens after salvation has taken place.**

It's like a person acquiring a classic old car. An old car will usually require some refurbishing. The purchaser of the car will buy the car as it is and bring it home to do the restoration later. This is exactly what God does for us; He claims us as his own and does touch-ups later. He makes us righteous by His sovereign will and our faith in Christ. He then surrenders us to the holiness process later.

If a Person Is Truly Born Again, There Will Be a Burning Desire to Express His Christianity Outwardly through His Lifestyle.

When one is sincerely born again, there will be a natural progression towards a manifestation in that person's behavior. What is on the inside will definitely seek to work its way to the outside. When the Apostle Paul addressed the Philippian Church he said, *"Wherefore, my beloved, as ye have always obeyed, not as in my presence only, but now much more in my absence, **work out your own salvation** with fear and trembling. For it is God which works in you both to will and to do of his good pleasure."* PHILIPPIANS 2:12–13

When a Person Has Had a Real Conversion Experience, God Immediately, by the Holy Spirit, Begins to Bring About a Holy Conviction.

He develops in us a will to do what pleases Him. The motivation for holy living has to run deeper than appearances and rituals.

The greatest motivation for holy living must not be fear of Hell or acceptance of religious people. **The truest motivation for holy living is grounded in one's love for God.** Jesus says in JOHN 14:15: *"If ye love me, keep my commandments."*

Our love for God is the only force that can consistently overcome the temptations of the flesh. Our commitment to holiness isn't the absence of sinful temptation; rather, it is the presence of the Holy Spirit overcoming our flesh. Francis Frangipane in his book, *Holiness Truth and the Presence of God,* states that *"holiness is not merely the absence of sin but it is the presence of God."* Without God's presence, there is no holiness.

The Only Permanent Antidote for Sinful
Flesh Is the Holy Presence Of God

FACT NUMBER FOUR ABOUT HOLINESS:
Worship and Holiness Are Inseparable.

The only possibility we have of living holy is to have the flesh under subjection. This is easier said than it is done, so how is this accomplished? The sad error many believers make is to assume that we can live holy of ourselves. We often attempt to do what only God can do in us and through us. What is even sadder is that we may even take credit for the work that God does in us.

Sometimes we begin to experience victory over certain areas of sin and rather than recognize that it's strictly God working in us; we give our flesh credit. The truth is that any person that lives a consistent lifestyle of holiness is simply dominated by God on a daily basis. It has little to do with the individual. The flesh is as vile as ever.

The only thing that keeps the flesh under control is God's abiding presence, and nothing else. The enemy understands this very well. Have you ever wondered why it is that you can hold a two-hour conversation and never get bored, while when it comes to praying, it's hard to focus for ten minutes? Why is it that we can stand up at football games for four hours, and get tired in a half-hour of corporate worship? Why is it that we can read novels for hours, and when we pick up the Word of God we instantly fall asleep? The answer is that the enemy works overtime to keep us from anything that draws us closer to God and enhances the presence of God upon our lives.

When We Live In God's Presence, the
Flesh Is Made Subject.

HABBAKKUK 2:20 says: *"But the LORD is in his holy temple: let all the earth keep silence before him."*

This text carries a very powerful revelation concerning the flesh and the presence of God. The *temple* in this text is symbolic of the child of God. The term *earth* is symbolic of the flesh nature and carnality. The revelation is this: **When we invoke the holy presence of God, the flesh is arrested and made subject.** Notice, when the presence of God shows up in His temple, the earth keeps silent. God's holy presence brings a holy hush to the voice of our flesh.

To Minimize the Flesh, Nature Requires
the Magnification of God.

There is an Old Testament story that carries some wonderful truth. It is found in 2 CHRONICLES and it says, *"It came even to pass, as the trumpeters and singers were as one, to make one sound to be heard in praising and thanking the LORD; and when they lifted up their voice with the trumpets and cymbals and instruments of music, and praised the LORD, saying, For He is good; for His mercy endureth for ever: that then the house was filled with a cloud, even the house of the LORD; So that the priests could not stand to minister by reason of the cloud: for the glory of the LORD had filled the house of God."* 2 CHRONICLES 5:13–14

Notice how the priest could not stand in the presence of God. The priests are symbolic of the flesh. This is very important in understanding how the presence of God empowers us to maintain a commitment to holy living.

The Most Effective Way to Rise Above the Sinful Pull of the Flesh Is to Stay Caught Up in the Presence of God.

When we live in the presence of God, the inclinations of flesh nature cannot dominate.

A Life-Changing Experience:

I was in my mid-twenties when I had an experience with God that forever changed my life. I was living in a one-bedroom apartment. That modest little apartment became the House of God. With all of my many years of going to church, I learned how to worship in that apartment. I was alone with God and His presence transformed me. It was in the intimacy of God's presence that transformation took place.

In the worship, the holiness of God began to rub off on my heart and nature. Suddenly I understood why Moses had to take off his shoes. It was not because the sin of Moses could affect God; but, God wanted His holiness to affect Moses. God wanted no barriers between Him and Moses. God wanted Moses to receive the full impartation of His character and nature. God wanted to rub off on Moses.

As you learn to worship, you will find it to be a transforming and life-altering experience. The psalmist put it in beautiful terms when he said, *"Thy testimonies are very sure: holiness becometh thine house, O LORD, for ever."* PSALM 93:5

Once we get into the presence of God through worship, His glory serves to further subdue the flesh and its weaknesses.

Daily Worship Is the Empowerment to
Stay Above the Flesh.

The practical application of this principle amounts to a few things. You must identify worship music that really ministers to your heart, and begin to spend time with God in worship. God will always meet you in the place of worship. You can do this in your car, taking your daily walk, or wherever. Involve God in your daily life. He will empower you to overcome your weaknesses.

SUMMARY OF CHAPTER TWO

1. Holiness must be taught before people will attain to it.
2. Spiritual leadership has a great effect on the quality of your lifestyle.
3. Holiness is our gift to God.
4. We don't live holy to be saved; we live holy because we are saved.
5. Righteousness and holiness aren't the same.
6. The Holy Spirit creates a desire for holiness.
7. Love for God drives our pursuit of holiness.
8. Daily worship is mandatory to overcoming the weaknesses of the flesh nature.

R.C.BLAKES, JR.

CHAPTER 3

THE RESPONSIBILITIES
OF HOLINESS

As a child I wanted to learn to swim. My dad told me that he could teach me to swim with just one lesson. I was excited about the thought of gliding through the water and being able to enjoy the many benefits of knowing how to swim. My dad explained to me how the lesson would go, and I quickly lost my enthusiasm. He said: *"I will take you to the pool and simply throw you into the deepest end."* I asked him what would happen after that, and he replied, in so many words, *"when your mind conceives that you must swim or drown, you will swim. When swimming is no longer a choice to make, but a necessity to live, you will swim."* I said no, thank you!

This childhood incident perfectly captures the approach that we must take towards holiness. Holiness is not a nice idea; it is a mandatory offering to our most worthy God. We owe Him at least this much. Holiness must not be perceived as optional. It must be perceived as a necessity. We will never commit to the process until we completely view it as imperative.

We Either Strive For Holiness or We Die! We Die Spiritually, Socially, and Sometimes We Die Physically When We View Holiness as an Option.

Take a look at society and its rapid decline. Values and respect for biblical morality are things of the past. All of this is a clarion call to return to God's way for living. It's the call of holiness.

There is a passage of scripture found in 2 CHRONICLES that serves as a general outline of everything we will discuss in this book. It says, *"If my people, which are called by my name, shall humble themselves, and pray, and seek my face, and turn from their wicked ways; then will I hear from heaven, and will forgive their sin, and will heal their land. Now mine eyes shall be open, and mine ears attend unto the prayer that is made in this place."* 2 CHRONICLES 7:14–15

This passage reveals three very important things concerning holiness. It reveals the responsibility we have as the people of God to the pursuit of holiness. It discloses some of the basic requirements to succeed in the process of holiness, and finally it unfolds the great global results of living for God.

The text starts off by addressing those who are called by God's name. **Being called by His name speaks**

of being identified with and related to God as His people. The underlying factor in this instance is that, those called by another's name are identified as being related to the individual.

If One Is Related There Should Be Some Resemblance.

In scripture, God's name always represents His nature or character. When God mentions those called by His name, it is indicating He is searching for those who would model His nature and character in the earth.

I have four children, and wherever they go, people know who their father is just by the way they look. We are supposed to be so much like God that the world can see Him in us.

We Have The Responsibility to
Represent God in the Earth.

The passage in 2 CHRONICLES goes on to address certain basic requirements that every child of God must meet. The nature of God should be revealed to the world by our lifestyle. We are the physical representatives of God to the world. This is a part of what Jesus meant when he called us "the light of the world."

The First Requirement Is That We Must Deny Our Flesh.

The second thing that 2 CHRONICLES 7 says to us is that we must humble ourselves. The Hebrew term for *humble* is *kana`* (kaw-nah'). It means to bring down, or to bring into subjection. When the Word says, "humble themselves," it is speaking of the fact that our flesh and pride must be purposely brought down. The mental picture is that of a wrestler subduing his opponent.

Living the Holiness Lifestyle Requires Refusing to Accommodate Your Flesh.

A cock trainer kept cocks and trained them for fighting. (By the way, I do not endorse such activity.) Every time there was a fight, the trainer could always tell which cock would win. A young man asked what his secret was, and the gentleman told him that he would not feed one cock for a day and a half while he would nourish the other. The unfed cock would always lose because he had no strength. **When we humble the flesh we take its strength from it, and it loses.**

The Bible gives great wisdom in this matter. It says: *"For if ye live after the flesh, ye shall die: but if ye through the Spirit do mortify the deeds of the body, ye shall live. For as many as are led by the Spirit of God, they are the sons of God."* ROMANS 8:13–14

The term *mortify* in this text is the Greek term *thanatoo* (than-at-o'-o). It means to kill, literally or figuratively. The greatest enemy we have working against the holiness process is our very own flesh nature. It must be purposely killed.

We Mortify (Kill) the Flesh Nature in at Least Three Specific Ways:

First: Refuse to Feed the Flesh What It Likes.

We feed the flesh by allowing ourselves to be found in certain anti-holiness settings and participating in certain behavior. Anything that promotes ungodliness has to be excised. It must be cut out of the lifestyle intentionally.

I have had a lifelong struggle to maintain my weight for most of my adulthood. It's a never-ending process. Over the years, I have discovered that the only way I can really beat the addiction to food is to simply oppose the desires of my appetite. If I starve the addiction, my mind eventually becomes stronger than the desire for the wrong foods.

Likewise, we must starve the flesh nature of the things that promote carnality and sin. The word of God puts it this way: *"But put ye on the Lord Jesus Christ, and make not provision for the flesh, to fulfill the lusts thereof."* ROMANS 13:14

Notice, the text says: *"don't make provision for the flesh."* It's simple; anything that nourishes flesh in your life has to go.

Second: Don't Allow Your Flesh to Have an Opinion.

We have to recognize the voice of our flesh when it is attempting to influence our behavior. We cannot entertain flesh at all. The word of God says, *"For we are the circumcision, which worship God in the spirit, and rejoice in Christ Jesus, and have no confidence in the flesh."* PHILIPPIANS 3:3

Third: Stay Built Up in the Things Of God.

If we are going to have the spiritual stamina to deny our flesh, we will have to have a strong spirit. This means that we have to gravitate to the things that make us strong spiritually. As Paul states in GALATIANS 5:16, *"This I say then, Walk in the Spirit, and ye shall not fulfill the lust of the flesh."*

Holiness Will Require the Constant
Nurturing of Your Spirit Man.

The text in 2 CHRONICLES 7 moves on to encourage the child of God to "pray." The admonishment to pray is the call to draw close to God in your spirit.

Holiness Cannot Happen Apart from God's Participation.

Contrary to popular religious thinking, we cannot be holy of ourselves. Look closely at the scripture as it states in JAMES 4:7–8 that says: *"Submit yourselves therefore to God. Resist the devil, and he will flee from you. Draw nigh to God, and he will draw nigh to you. Cleanse your hands, ye sinners; and purify your hearts, ye double minded."*

This text points to the fact that God's presence precedes holiness. Notice how the text states that we should draw close to God and afterwards we should cleanse our hands. Hands represent our deeds or actions, but the cleansing doesn't take place until we draw nigh to God.

Cleansing happens in the presence of God. The scripture says: *"This I say then, Walk in the Spirit, and ye shall not fulfill the lust of the flesh."* GALATIANS 5:16

Holiness Will Require Turning Your Back on
Your Old Way of Living.

Our base text in 2 CHRONICLES 7 goes on to say: *"repent."* Repent does not merely mean to be sorry. *It means to be sorry and to turn around and go in the opposite direction.*

When a person repents they go in a different direction. If you were supposed to be going west and happened to be heading east, it would not be enough to just be sorry that you were heading in the wrong direction. You would have to stop, turn around, and adjust your direction. The call to repent is the call to depart from any way that does not line up with God's will.

ISAIAH 55:6–7 says: *"Seek ye the LORD while he may be found, call ye upon him while he is near: Let the wicked forsake his way, and the unrighteous man his thoughts."*

The prophet Isaiah is encouraging the people to forsake their wicked ways and thoughts. To forsake means *to abandon without care for.* The holiness lifestyle requires an aggressive departure from the old life and total commitment to the new and living way.

Holiness Will Require a Constant Hunger for God.

The 2 CHRONICLES 7 passage finally instructs us to *"seek God's face."* This speaks of developing an honest desire for an intimate fellowship with God. To seek God's face is to desire to really know Him, not for what He can do, but for who He is. We will never come into holiness until we desire God more than anything else. This is why the Bible says, *"Blessed are they which do hunger and thirst after righteousness: for they shall be filled."* MATTHEW 5:6

When we hunger for God, we will ultimately be filled with Him.

Holiness Is Simply Being so Full of God That He Shines Through.

There's a story my father often told in his sermons. It's the story of a young preacher who asked his pastor what it meant to hunger for God. The seasoned pastor took the young man out into the middle of a lake in a rowboat. When they arrived at the deepest point, the pastor asked the young man to get out of the boat. When he did, the pastor proceeded to lean over the side of the boat and to hold the young man's head beneath the water. The young man kicked violently. When the pastor finally let him up he said to the young man, "now you know what it means to hunger for God." The young man begged an explanation. The pastor said, "When you have to have God as much as you just had to have air, then and only then will you find Him."

As We Fulfill the Requirements of Holiness,
God Begins to Bring Healing to Certain Areas of Life.

In 2 CHRONICLES 7, God says: *"when His people understand the responsibility to live for Him, and meet the basic requirements, the result would be the healing of the land."* The healing of the land speaks of God moving upon the landscape and rectifying the many ailments that the withdrawal from God's ways has brought about. **When men live like God commands, the blessings of God take over.** When men disobey God's commands, curses persist. The scripture says: *"If ye be willing and obedient, ye shall eat the good of the land."* ISAIAH 1:19

SUMMARY OF CHAPTER THREE

1. We are responsible to look like God.
2. Holiness requires denying the flesh.
3. Holiness requires nurturing your spirit man.
4. Holiness requires forsaking your old lifestyle.
5. Holiness requires desiring God more.
6. When we offer God a holy life, He responds by healing the land.

R.C.BLAKES, JR.

SECTION B

HOW
DOES HOLINESS WORK?

CHAPTER 4

UNDERSTANDING
THE FLESH NATURE

Have you ever encountered a Christian that seemed so spiritual that you had to wonder if they even needed oxygen or water? It's humorous to observe certain believers who act as though they don't have any idea what the flesh nature is all about.

If we would follow some of these super spiritual saints to their favorite restaurant and watch the mountain of carbohydrates they consume, it would become obvious that they really do have a flesh nature. Others can sit in front of a television screen from morning until night. These are some common and less destructive appetites of the flesh nature, but nonetheless flesh. The flesh can also utilize these same influential strategies to generate far more destructive behaviors. We must be aware of the flesh nature in order to manage it.

There Are Three Dimensions to Man's Makeup and They All Work against Each Other.

A common error many Christians make is to think that we are only spiritual. There is much more to you than what is spiritual. You are made up of spirit, soul (mind), and body.

In the book of Genesis, when God made Adam, He formed him from the dust of the ground. This represented his body. God breathed into his nostrils and Adam became a living soul. When God breathed into Adam, two things happened simultaneously. He became mentally aware, speaking of his soul; and he became spiritually alive. He had an awareness and communion with his creator. Adam was made body, soul, and spirit.

The word of God says in I THESSALONIANS 5:23 *"And the very God of peace sanctify you wholly; and I pray God your whole spirit and soul and body be preserved blameless unto the coming of our Lord Jesus Christ."*

Notice the reference to spirit, soul, and body. Man is a three-part being. Man is a spirit, he has a soul (mind), and he lives in a body.

The Body

The body is the physical external shell of man. The body makes man relatable to physical things. Without a body, man could have no relationship to the physical world. The body serves the same purpose for man that a spacesuit serves for an astronaut when in outer space. If the astronaut did not have the spacesuit, he could not exist in that atmosphere. If we did not have bodies, we could not occupy the earth legally. This is why Jesus had to have a body. He was born of a woman and made of flesh. The scripture says, *"That which is born of the flesh is flesh; and that which is born of the Spirit is spirit."* JOHN 3:6

The Soul/Mind

The soul is the center of reasoning, thinking, and decision-making. The soul is simply the mind. The condition of the soul makes man self-conscious and determines man's well-being and state of existence. The status of the soul determines the direction and quality of the individual's life. According to 3 JOHN 2, the Bible says: *"Beloved, I wish above all things that thou mayest prosper and be in health, even as thy soul prospereth."*

The Prosperity of the Soul Is the Key to Maximizing Life.

If the mind is weak, the life will be weak. If the mind is poor, the person's existence will be poor.

The Spirit

The spirit is the part of man that is God-conscious. The spirit relates to the things of God. The spirit of man is the part that responds to salvation and senses the presence of God.

The Spirit Is the Part of Man
That God Communicates With.

As PROVERBS 20:27 says: *"The spirit of man is the candle of the LORD, searching all the inward parts of the belly."*

Notice how the writer uses an interesting illustration that we can all identify with. He says that the spirit of man serves as a candle. A candle illuminates dark areas. When the text calls the spirit of man the candle of the Lord, it simply means that God can only shine light into our lives by way of our spirits.

The Spirit Is the Part of You and Me
That Desires the Will of God All the Time.

This is the part of your being that desires to pray all the time. Your spirit is the part of your being that is born again and is God-conscious.

The conflict is that there is a great warfare between the spirit, which desires God's will, and the flesh nature, which always desires the opposite of God's will. The soul is in the middle of it all.

Salvation Does Not Eliminate Your Flesh Nature.

Salvation gives us access to a higher nature, which is God's nature. However, if we don't learn how to activate the higher nature, the flesh (lower nature) will continue to dominate our lives as if we are not even saved. You and I both have a flesh nature. If we don't subdue the flesh nature, it will cause us to perform just like we did before we were born again.

The Apostle Paul was confused when he discovered that his conversion did not eliminate his flesh nature. Even though he was saved and called to the ministry, he still had a problem with his flesh. Just like Paul, I also thought that salvation eliminated my flesh. I soon learned that the opposite is true; **once you are saved, the pull of your flesh nature actually becomes greater.**

Satan intensifies his appeal to your fleshly tendencies to keep you from surrendering to the Spirit of God. Some of the tendencies of the flesh are revealed in the fifth chapter of Galatians. It says, *"Now the works of the flesh are manifest, which are these; Adultery, fornication, uncleanness, lasciviousness, idolatry, witchcraft, hatred, variance, emulations, wrath, strife, seditions, heresies."* GALATIANS 5:19–20

Many in the Body of Christ are not very comfortable with the statement that I am about to make, but it is the truth.

Everything Mentioned in Galatians 5:19–20 Is Prevalent among Born Again Saints and Even Leaders.

Is it because people don't want to do better? Not in most cases. In most cases, people actually desire to live for God but find it problematic to reconcile their desires with their behavior.

What Is the Problem?

The problem arises basically as a result of simple ignorance. The church does very little teaching on the subject of holiness, and people don't fully understand the flesh nature and its traps. One of the first rules of effective combat is to know the strengths and weaknesses of your enemy.

Your Flesh Is the Enemy of Holiness. You Cannot Maximize the Holy Potential of Your Born-Again Spirit until You Embrace an Understanding of Your Flesh Nature.

It does not matter who you are or what position you hold in the church, you, too, have a flesh nature. The sooner you come to this realization, the sooner you can take control of your life. We can't be like the ostrich and stick our heads in the sand when the enemy comes, hoping that the enemy will go away. You cannot ignore the flesh because it will take you out.

ROMANS 5:12 says: *"Wherefore, as by one man sin entered into the world, and death by sin; and so death passed upon all men, for that all have sinned."* The death this text is speaking of is not physical extinction. It is a separation from God. It's a spiritual death.

Adam knew what it was to be in sync with God. He thought God's thoughts and felt God's presence. When Adam disobeyed he lost all of that. He could not hear God's voice or feel His presence; he became spiritually dead. **When there's a death to the things of God in your life, it increases the tendency to yield to the leading of the flesh.** It might help to think of it this way: If you suddenly lost the feeling in one of your hands, you would automatically become increasingly dependent on the other hand.

When A Christian Is De-Sensitized to the Things
of God, the Flesh Becomes Dominant.

63

When your flesh dominates you, it's automatic that Satan gains an advantage over you. This is why people who are flesh-led tend to do things even when they don't really want to. **This is one major distinction between being spirit-led versus flesh-led: God leads you, as you willfully surrender to Him** (spirit-led). **Satan, on the other hand, dominates you through the weaknesses of your flesh against your will** (flesh-led).

Paul refers to the flesh nature in the book of Romans. Paul says, *"But I see another law in my members, warring against the law of my mind, and bringing me into captivity to the law of sin which is in my members. O wretched man that I am! Who shall deliver me from the body of this death?"* ROMANS 7:23–24

Notice Paul says that he was brought into captivity to the law of sin. This denotes an unwillingness on his part. He also acknowledges that this law is in his members (mind and body). Paul is making us aware that this is a force that is coming from within him. Why? He was born with it!

Think about it. We have to teach babies to share and to tell the truth; we don't have to teach them to fight, to lie, or to steal. Why? It's programmed in their flesh nature when they get here.

This discussion obviously leads to a serious question. **Why is the flesh nature so dominant in the life of a Christian?** The first reason the flesh nature is so dominant in some Christians' lives is because it is the oldest and most familiar nature. It's like anything in life; we always revert back to what is habitual, familiar, or rehearsed. We were born with the flesh nature; we were conceived in the flesh. It is what we've always known.

1 CORINTHIANS 15:46 says: *"How be it that was not first which is spiritual, but that which is natural; and afterward that which is spiritual."*

You and I were born into this. It wasn't our choice; however, we do have a choice as to if it dominates us or not.

The reason we need to be born again is to offset the dominion of the flesh nature. It makes sense; if you want a new nature you need a new birth. **Your first birth was natural and transferred to you the flesh nature with all of its predispositions and desires. When you were born again, by faith in Jesus Christ, you received a new nature, from God.** It is the born-again nature that gives you the potential to over-ride the older nature of the flesh.

The Flesh Is Dominant Because It Has Been

with You All of Your Life.

The second reason the flesh nature is as dominant is because it has an open line of communication with Satan. The flesh is sensitive to Satan's voice. The word says: "*Ye are of your father the devil, and the lusts of your father ye will do. He was a murderer from the beginning, and abode not in the truth, because there is no truth in him. When he speaketh a lie, he speaketh of his own: for he is a liar, and the father of it.*" JOHN 8:44

The Flesh Nature Is Submissive to the Voice of Satan Because It Views Him as Its Father.

Satan is the father of the flesh because he caused the first man, Adam, to fall from his lofty place of dominion and glory through disobedience.

When Adam Disobeyed God, His Spirit Became Deafened to the Voice of God and His Flesh Was Awakened to Satan's Voice.

Consequently, the flesh is programmed to hear the voice of Satan; the voice of God is foreign to the flesh. It would be like a natural parent having her child kidnapped at birth and the child grows with the kidnappers. Years later, when the legitimate parent finds the child, the child will have no connection.

You Can Never Obey God in Your Flesh Alone.

The word of God declares, *"Because the carnal mind is enmity against God: for it is not subject to the law of God, neither indeed can be. So then they that are in the flesh cannot please God."* ROMANS 8:7

The term *enmity* simply means that the carnal mind is at war with God. When the text states that the carnal mind is not subject to the law of God, it means that it is incapable of understanding or responding to God's standards for living. He finishes the text by stating: *"they that are in the flesh cannot please God."* We must find a way to rise above the flesh to please God. It will not happen in the flesh.

When We Come to Christ We Receive a New Spirit from God.

When I was a kid growing up in the old Baptist Church, there was a song the choir would sing on Sunday morning that stated: *"I looked at my hands and my hands looked new, I looked at my feet and they did too."* That song was in reference to salvation and the supposed change that takes place when a person gives his heart to Christ. Well, that song was merely an expression of figurative language. The reality is that nothing changes on a person physically at conversion.

Nothing changes on the outside, but something tremendous happens on the inside at conversion. God places a new spirit within you. This new spirit is direct from God and creates new desires that you have never experienced before. You begin to actually feel bad about certain things that once would not faze you. This is the power of conviction fighting that old flesh nature.

EZEKIEL 36:26 says: *"A new heart also will I give you, and a new spirit will I put within you: and I will take away the stony heart out of your flesh, and I will give you a heart of flesh."*

This new spirit is aligned with God, and through the new spirit God communicates and fellowships with man. Just like the flesh nature is sensitive to Satan's voice, the new spirit is only sensitive to the voice of God. When you are saved, it is as if God re-establishes communication with you again. After salvation it's like it was before the first man, Adam, messed up. You are dead to the voice of God before you are born again. At conversion, the lines of communication are re-opened.

It Is Very Important to Remember That Being Born Again Does Not Cancel the Old Nature. It Only Means That There Are Now Two Conflicting Natures Residing within You.

Your new, born-again spirit begins to contend with the old carnal nature and creates an internal war zone. There becomes a struggle between the will of God and the desires of the flesh nature.

When God Says Yes, the Flesh Will Say No All the Time!

According to GALATIANS 5:17, the Bible says: *"For the flesh lusteth against the Spirit, and the Spirit against the flesh: and these are contrary the one to the other: so that ye cannot do the things that ye would."*

This writer reveals the fact that there is no hope of ever reconciling the flesh and the spirit. They will always work to overrule one another. Since our objective is to be spirit-led and not flesh-driven, the question presents itself: How do we position ourselves for the spirit to win the internal struggle?

The Nature That Is Fed the Most Will Dominate.

Whichever side is catered to and fed the most will dominate your life. If you spend your time gratifying your flesh, your flesh will be stronger and tyrannize your life. If you cater to your spirit man, he will be stronger and give the orders. It's really as simple as that. Whichever is stronger will control matters.

I remember as a child, my younger brother and I would fight quite often. I would always win because I was older, bigger, and stronger. I had been here longer so I had an edge in the strength department. My brother did not make much noise but he kept doing what was necessary to get bigger and stronger. He kept on eating and growing. One day, I can so well remember, I started a fight with him and he was suddenly stronger and faster than I was. Once I realized that I was no longer dominant, I quickly screamed: "The Lord is not pleased with all of this fighting. We must stop this senseless violence amongst brothers!" It was not so much the Lord as it was that right hook he threw at me. He was now stronger than me and I could no longer dominate.

This same thing is true in the struggle between your flesh and your spirit.

Even Though Your Flesh Nature May Be Older and Stronger Initially, If You Faithfully Feed Your Spirit Man He Will Become Stronger and More Dominant in Your Life.

The carnal nature feeds off of natural things like television, carnal conversation, and other natural stimuli. The spirit man must be fed the word of God, Godly fellowship, worship, and anything else that glorifies God.

The word of God says, *"And have put on the new man, which is renewed in knowledge after the image of him that created him."* COLOSSIANS 3:10

Notice the word *renew* in this passage. It is the Greek term *anakainoo.* It means *to cause to grow up, to make new, to give new strength and vigor.*

When we give the spirit man a constant diet of God's word, he begins to grow up and gain new strength. As we feed him the word, he starts to dominate the territory of our lives.

You Must Desire God as Much as You Once
Desired the World.

In an earlier chapter, we talked about how the word of God declares: *"He that hungers and thirsts for righteousness shall be filled."* It is only when we truly experience a hunger for God that we will experience the desire that bends us towards the things that will produce His nature.

Once again, this passage in the book of Romans shines some light on this very important truth. It says, *"I speak after the manner of men because of the infirmity of your flesh: for as ye have yielded your members servants to uncleanness and to iniquity unto iniquity; even so now yield your members servants to righteousness unto holiness."* ROMANS 6:19

Most Believers Never Genuinely Yield
Themselves to the Things of God.

This is why all over America, bible study and
prayer meetings are nearly empty, while the theaters and
the malls are packed with Christians. *To yield means to
stop fighting or resisting. It means to give in.*

To Strengthen Your Spirit Man Will Require Placing
Yourself in the Position to Experience Spiritual Growth.

There must be a basic desire to overcome the flesh
nature. We must run after the things of the Spirit if we
would see the things of the Spirit manifested.

Think about the energy and commitment we all
had in pursuing the things of the world. If we put that
kind of energy into satisfying the flesh, how much more
should we do in pursuit of the holy things of Godliness?

One of our greatest hurdles is to come to terms
with the fact that the pursuit of God usually requires
separation from some old familiar things and people. Too
many believers think that they can keep the same
hangouts as they seek to change their hang-ups.

We Cannot Stay Under Fleshly Influences and Hope to

Produce Godly Character.

When God set me free from a totally lascivious (out of control) lifestyle, I had to disconnect from everything that related to that old way of living. I had to formulate new friendships, create new boundaries for living, change phone numbers, read different books, and even listen to different music to elevate the influence of God over the strength of my old flesh nature. I had to do these things on purpose.

This is why the book of Romans says, *"For they that are after the flesh do mind the things of the flesh; but they that are after the Spirit, the things of the Spirit. For to be carnally minded is death; but to be spiritually minded is life and peace."* ROMANS 8:5–6

Holiness must be intentionally and systematically pursued. The people that facilitated a fleshly mindset, in me, had to be dismissed from my life. It wasn't always easy but it was necessary for me to be who I am today. The Grace of God Will Help You to Overcome the Flesh.

When I was a child, we sang a great deal about grace. As I look back on it, I realize that we didn't have a clue as to how deep the river of grace runs. Grace is so misunderstood. **Grace is more than a passport out of Hell.** The grace of God plays a great role in effective Christian living. In fact, God has given us grace to begin the process of overcoming the flesh.

The Word of God says in EPHESIANS 2:7–10:

"That in the ages to come he might shew the exceeding riches of his grace in his kindness toward us through Christ Jesus. For by grace are ye saved through faith; and that not of yourselves: it is the gift of God: Not of works, lest any man should boast. For we are his workmanship, created in Christ Jesus unto good works, which God hath before ordained that we should walk in them."

Notice the text says that "we are saved by grace." To begin to gain a thorough understanding of this text we must acquire a complete definition of the term saved.

In Greek it's the term *sozo*. It means *to save, make whole, heal, and be whole.* It means *to save, keep safe and sound, to rescue from danger or destruction.* It also means *to deliver.*

The main word is *deliver.* **Deliverance in the life of a child of God is multi-faceted. Deliverance is past, present, and future.**

In Sunday School they taught us that we have been delivered from the penalty of sin; that's past tense. We are being delivered from the power of sin. That's present tense. We will one day, at the return of our Lord, be delivered from the very presence of sin. That is future tense. I always thought about salvation only in terms of going to Heaven one day. The truth is that our salvation is at work on a daily basis; most just don't know it.

Salvation Is Not Just about Eternity; Salvation Is Also the Daily Deliverance from the Many Vices of the Flesh.

Listen to the words of Jesus: *"Come unto me, all ye that labour and are heavy laden, and I will give you rest. Take my yoke upon you, and learn of me; for I am meek and lowly in heart: and ye shall find rest unto your souls. For my yoke is easy, and my burden is light."*
MATTHEW 11:28–30

An excellent mental picture of this text would be that of a man carrying around a wagon marked flesh, and it's filled with heavy bricks. Think of how difficult it would be to make progress carrying that kind of weight; suddenly, Jesus comes along and makes an offer to pull the wagon for him. When he allows Christ to pull the weight, in return, Christ gives him rest from the struggle.

Also notice the text starts with the word *"come."* The point is that God is waiting on us to meet Him on His terms. Once we do, He'll do the rest.

Salvation Is Not a One-Moment-In-A-Lifetime Experience.

It Is a Perpetual Experience That Affords the Believer a
Lifetime of Deliverance and Growth from
One Level to the Next.

According to EPHESIANS 2:8, we are delivered by
grace. **Grace is the power that enables us to overcome
the flesh.** Grace is the benevolence of God by which He
influences our minds to turn to Christ. This same
influence keeps and strengthens the believer. God will
also use this same influence to increase the child of God
in the Christian faith, knowledge, and affections. **Grace is
simply God giving us His power to live with.**

Grace Is The Power That Brings Us to Christ and Keeps
Us in Christ While It Perfects His Divine Nature
in Us as We Live.

The Word says: *"But grow in grace, and in the
knowledge of our Lord and Savior Jesus Christ. To him be
glory both now and for ever. Amen."* 2 PETER 3:18

Notice the writer says, *"grow in grace."* Growth
implies progress and the strengthening of something.
Grace is not a scapegoat to get out of meeting God's
standards. It's quite the opposite; it's the power to get it
done.

Grace Should Produce Growth, Not Complacency.

The church has used grace as a crutch to be weak. This was not God's intention! Grace was never designed to be a license to stagnate your spiritual development. It is to be an empowerment to advance spiritually. Grace is the gift of God's ability working in us and for us.

The Apostle Paul writes to the church at Corinth and says: *"And lest I should be exalted above measure through the abundance of the revelations, there was given to me a thorn in the flesh, the messenger of Satan to buffet me, lest I should be exalted above measure. For this thing I besought the Lord thrice, that it might depart from me. And he said unto me, My grace is sufficient for thee: for my strength is made perfect in weakness. Most gladly therefore will I rather glory in my infirmities, that the power of Christ may rest upon me. Therefore I take pleasure in infirmities, in reproaches, in necessities, in persecutions, in distresses for Christ's sake: for when I am weak, then am I strong."* 2 CORINTHIANS 12:7–10

Paul had some sort of problem in his flesh. The scripture never specifies what the problem was, however God reveals to him that His grace, working in Paul, would be sufficient to overcome whatever the flesh was bringing against him. Paul wanted to handle the situation on his own, but God wanted him to know that He was working with him.

The Most Debilitating Misconception Pertaining to Holiness Is That We Do It without God's Help.

The Bible never asks us to be like God without God's help. The Bible says in the book of Philippians: *"For it is God which worketh in you both to will and to do of his good pleasure."* PHILIPPIANS 2:13

It is God's grace that gives us the initial desire to live for Him and it will be that same grace that will bring it to fruition. When we realize that we have the grace to live for God, we are elevated out of our hopelessness and weaknesses and into His strength. The idea that God is assisting me to live for Him is an amazing thought.

Grace is strength to do what we can't. Notice Ephesians 2:8 says: *"by grace are ye saved,"* or delivered, *"through faith."* Notice that this deliverance takes place through faith. **Faith is the ignition of grace.** It takes a total confidence in God, to access the power of grace to keep you.

You Must Believe That God Will Keep You Before He Will.

Paul wrote to the young pastor Timothy and said: *"For the which cause I also suffer these things: nevertheless I am*

not ashamed: for I know whom I have believed, and am persuaded that he is able to keep that which I have committed unto him against that day."
2 TIMOTHY 1:12

In this passage Paul says to Timothy that he is persuaded that God is able to keep whatever is committed to Him. **We must commit our lives to God and trust Him to do the rest.** It takes faith to release the power of God's grace, to empower you to live for him.

For a long time, I didn't believe I could be kept. I didn't see anyone around me who was being kept. I wanted to do right but I never seemed to be able to perform what I desired. My faith was very low concerning the possibility of being kept by God.

I lived like this until the Lord changed my father's life. I had been accustomed to my dad being a drinking preacher. My dad was once an actual alcoholic. I felt justified in my failure because it was all I had ever seen. My father's testimony was that God delivered him from alcoholism and filled him with the Holy Spirit. He suddenly gave up drinking and his ministry catapulted to unbelievable heights. He was preaching with a new conviction. I was never accustomed to him preaching and living the same thing. At first I thought that this new lifestyle of his was a passing phase. Finally, it occurred to me that this phase had lasted for years, and his commitment was getting stronger. At this point, I was faced with a startling possibility; maybe God could keep a person in the way of holiness? Suddenly I had new hope. I had a living example before my eyes and I began to believe in the possibility of holiness.

It Is Important to Have Holy Examples Before You.

The word of God encourages us to follow those who are attaining to our aspirations. The writer of Hebrews says: *"That ye be not slothful, but followers of them who through faith and patience inherit the promises."* HEBREWS 6:12

As I followed the righteous example of my father, I simultaneously learned that this lifestyle was not possible in my own ability. It would only be possible in the ability of Christ. It was a revelation to me that Christ could actually live His life through me. All I needed to do was to allow Him to take over. My father would often say, "God has to live through you."

The Only Way Christ Comes Alive in
Us Is When We Die.

We must decrease as He increases. We must be crucified in terms of our will, our emotions, and our desires.

GALATIANS 2:20 says: *"I am crucified with Christ: nevertheless I live; yet not I, but Christ liveth in me: and the life which I now live in the flesh I live by the faith of the Son of God, who loved me, and gave himself for me."*

SUMMARY OF CHAPTER FOUR

1. Man is a three-part being: spirit, soul, and body.
2. The spirit of man is God conscious. The soul is the mind and self-consciousness. The body is the physical and world consciousness of man.
3. The spirit of man is the only part that God communes with.
4. Being saved does not eliminate the desires of the flesh nature.
5. The flesh nature is initially more dominant because you were born with it and it's been with you all of your life.
6. When we come to Christ, he puts a new spirit in us that reaches for God.
7. The flesh and the spirit will never agree, and the soul is in the middle.
8. The nature that is fed the most will dominate.
9. We cannot stay under fleshly influences and produce Godly character.

10. God's grace is His ability working in us.

CHAPTER 5

HOLINESS IS A PROCESS

As a young single man, I remember purchasing an inexpensive entertainment center. I brought it home in a big box. When I opened it there were what looked like a thousand pieces. The instructions were clearly displayed on top of the contents; however, I chose to do a freelance job. When I finished, my entertainment center was complete, but it was very unstable. I had to brace it in a corner, against a wall, to prevent it from falling down.

Some weeks later, my brother decided that he wanted one of these very same entertainment centers. I strongly encouraged him to avoid trying to put it together himself. He took my advice and sought the assistance of a certain relative of ours who is skilled in matters requiring tools.

When his entertainment center was complete, it was stable and secure. It seemed as though it was assembled for a lifetime of service. I was so puzzled at the difference between his and mine, I had to ask the gentleman that did the work what he did differently. As he explained what he had done, I soon realized my error. I did not follow the instructions, and consequently I confused much of the process and even eliminated certain parts of the process. My impatience and failure to follow the process resulted in a faulty product.

In this chapter we will explore the fact that there's a fundamental process to living the holiness lifestyle, and impatience must be avoided. This fact is beautifully demonstrated with the Old Testament priest. These priests went through a distinct consecration process for their priestly occupations. This consecration ceremony was an extensive process that lasted as long as seven days. This is important to us, because we are also priests unto the Lord, and the things of the Old Testament are simply examples to us in this New Testament dispensation (time).

The Old Testament is nothing but New Testament lessons concealed or hidden, waiting to be recognized.

There Is a Direct Correlation Between Our Process of Holiness and the Consecration Process of the Old Testament Priest.

We find a reference to the consecration of Old Testament priests in the book of Exodus. It says: *"And this is the thing that thou shalt do unto them to hallow them, to*

minister unto me in the priest's office: Take one young
bullock, and two rams without blemish. And unleavened
bread, and cakes unleavened tempered with oil, and wafers
unleavened anointed with oil: of wheaten flour shalt thou
make them. And thou shalt put them into one basket, and
bring them in the basket, with the bullock and the two rams.
And Aaron and his sons thou shalt bring unto the door of the
tabernacle of the congregation, and shalt wash them with
water. And thou shalt take the garments, and put upon
Aaron the coat, and the robe of the ephod, and the ephod,
and the breastplate, and gird him with the curious girdle of
the ephod: And thou shalt put the mitre upon his head, and
put the holy crown upon the mitre. Then shalt thou take the
anointing oil, and pour it upon his head, and anoint him."
EXODUS 29:1–7

The Lord's instruction was to hallow the priest. The
term *hallow* is the Hebrew term *qadash (kaw-dash').* It
means *to cause to be clean or to be purified.* It was the work
of consecrating the persons whom God had selected to be
priests. This consecration ceremony declared two things.

First: *It was an announcement on behalf of the*
priests that they had devoted and given themselves totally
to God's service.

Secondly: *It was a heavenly announcement of*
God's acceptance of the priests.

The priests were to be men who occupied a distinguished position with God and within society. Their role was not commonplace among men. This is meaningful to us because today we have too many commonplace Christians. Sometimes it's difficult to distinguish between saints and sinners. Note: All that are to be in the service of God are to be hallowed to Him.

Matthew Henry's Commentary says: *"the person must first be accepted, and then the performance."*

We must walk on the earth with the understanding that we are to carry ourselves as the holy vessels of God. Many times, as believers, we find ourselves in certain places in society where we are pressured to behave in a common fashion. For instance, barbershops and beauty parlors have a tendency to pull the worst out of some Christians. It matters not where we are; we must remember that we are to be sanctified unto the Lord as His vessels.

For the Old Testament priest, the place of consecration was at the door of the tabernacle. *There's a great purpose in this. God's presence dwelt inside the tabernacle. The people were in the courts or on the outside. The door was between the court and the tabernacle. The priest had the unique vocation of going between God and men. With one hand the priest touched*

God, and with the other hand they touched men. They were consecrated at the door, for they were to be doorkeepers. What is the significance?

We, Too Stand between God and Man and Our Consecration Ought to Be in View of God and the People We Touch for Him.

One of the biggest hindrances to the Christian witness is a person whose talk and walk don't match. People should see our consecration manifested before their eyes.

Our Consecration Ought to Be Visible to All.

I remember going to a certain restaurant whose preparation area was visually exposed. As I perused the area, I noticed that the counters and floors were filthy. I observed that the cooks had unusually soiled clothes and aprons. Their impurities were so obvious that I lost my appetite for their menu. This perfectly captures the necessity of the Christian's public sanctity. If the world looks upon our lives and fails to find us in a consecrated state, they will reject our message. Mind you, I did not expect that restaurant's cooking area to be as sterile as an operating room, but at least it should have looked like somebody cleaned up periodically.

The World Does Not Expect Us to Be Flawless, but They Do Expect Us to Appear as If We Are Working at It.

The people in the Old Testament had a great respect for the priest because the people saw the great price they paid to serve in such a capacity. As it relates to our New Testament walk, we must understand that there is a price to pay to live for God. There's a comparison to the physical process of the Old Testament priest and our process today. Let us begin to take a brief look at the consecration processes of the Old Testament priests.

In EXODUS 29:4 it says: *"And Aaron and his sons thou shalt bring unto the door of the tabernacle of the congregation, and shalt wash them with water."*

The Priests Were to Be Washed.

The priest physically washed himself. **For us, the washing denotes that those who will come in and out of the presence of the Lord must be clean.** One of the most awful fallouts of sin is that it keeps us out of the presence of God. Those who bear the vessels of the Lord in service must be purged.

According to Isaiah, the word of God says, *"Depart ye, depart ye, go ye out from thence, touch no* unclean thing; go ye out of the midst of her; be ye clean, that bear the vessels of the LORD." ISAIAH 52:11

Those that would seek to perfect holiness must cleanse themselves from all filthiness of flesh and spirit. Cleansing is obviously very important, but the question is, how are we cleansed today? I'm glad you asked. The cleansing of the New Testament believer transcends the process of the Old Testament priest. The Old Testament priest experienced an external purifying, but the New Testament believer experiences a cleansing that happens beneath the surface. It is the purification of the heart. How does it happen?

The Word says, "Now ye are clean through the word which I have spoken unto you." JOHN 15:3

The cleansing of the New Testament believer happens as we submit ourselves to the word of God. **The word is our detergent and it must not be diluted with religious opinions, and men-pleasing additions.** The opinions of men can never cleanse. I have seen many believers who were suffering with all kinds of vices, and I've noticed something: *The opinions of a thousand church members will not change the behavior of one individual; however, when the Word of God is effectively and consistently administered it does the purifying.*

The Priests Were to Be Clothed with Holy Garments.

The Word of God says in Exodus: *"And thou shalt take the garments, and put upon Aaron the coat, and the robe of the ephod, and the ephod, and the breastplate, and gird him with the curious girdle of the ephod: And thou shalt put the mitre upon his head, and put the holy crown upon the mitre."* EXODUS 29:5

The new clothing signified that it was not acceptable to simply put off sin; they had to proceed to put on the things of God. *After the washing comes the clothing.* It would be unacceptable to take a bath and put on the same dirty clothes. A clean person should put on fresh clothing.

If You Don't Put on Fresh Clothing You Will
Look and Smell like You're Not Clean.

The priest put on special garments. The Bible states in PSALM 132:9, *"Let thy priests be clothed with righteousness; and let thy saints shout for joy."*

Every noble occupation requires a certain dress code. The police department has a uniform. The fire department has a uniform. There's an acceptable dress code to work on Capitol Hill. Likewise, the priests of the most high God have a particular spiritual dress code. Let's take a look at the attire of the priests as they were described in Exodus, Chapter 28. *The following information regarding the garments of the priests comes from the Wycliffe Bible Commentary:*

"The Ephod was the First Part of Clothing.
This was the most distinct piece of the priest's wardrobe. It was a sort of waist-length coat and it was elaborately tailored. It consisted of two pieces, front and back, joined at the shoulders by straps or shoulder pieces, and bound around the waist by a girdle that was part of the ephod itself. The ephod was considered to be the prayer garment. We, as New Testament believers, must be sure to clothe ourselves with the garment of prayer. Prayer is mandatory in obtaining and maintaining a sanctified lifestyle.

The Breastplate was the Second Piece.
The breastplate or "pouch" of judgment was a bag of the same material as the ephod. It was made of one piece of material, folded over to form a pouch, nine by nine inches. Note, this plate covered the heart of the priest.

The Urim and Thummim were the Third Pieces.
These two Hebrew words speak of lights and perfection. The real meaning cannot be determined with certainty, either from the names themselves or from any

other circumstances connected with them. It is believed
that this particular aspect of the vesture served the
purpose of the priests seeking and knowing God's will in
times of crisis. This applies to the New Testament believer
in that we must master the spirit of discernment. To live
for God is largely dependent on being able to know
God's will from one's own mind or satanic influences.
The Fourth Piece was the Robe of the Ephod.
It was woven from one piece of cloth and worn under the
ephod. Around the edge of the skirt were small golden
bells and pomegranates of twisted yarn. The bells
represent the sound of one's witness. The pomegranates
symbolize fruit-bearing and divine productivity.

The Fifth Part was the Headdress.
The headdress of the high priest was made of fine
white linen. The front of the headdress contained the
words "Holy to Jehovah." This could be compared to the
necessity of the New Testament saint having his mind
renewed to the things of God.

The Sixth Part of the Dress was the Tunic.
The tunic was designed in a check pattern and was
also made of linen. It was worn close to the body,
beneath the robe of the ephod.

Please notice that the holy garments covered the entire
body and went from the head to the toes. How does this

relate to our process? This signifies that we cannot attempt to enter the holiness of God partially. We must invest our whole selves. This life will require a total commitment."

These descriptions of the various aspects of the holy garments of the priests is taken from the Wycliffe Bible Commentary.

The High Priest Was Anointed with the Holy Anointing Oil.

The third major act in the consecration ceremony of the priest was to anoint the priest with oil. The Bible says in EXODUS 29:7: *"Then shalt thou take the anointing oil, and pour it upon his head, and anoint him."* This was special oil strictly used for anointing holy things. It wasn't common cooking oil or table oil. This oil was very special and specifically prepared for this purpose. Oil was used to consecrate people and things to the holy and divine purposes of God.

The oil used to set the priest aside was a type of our New Testament in-filling of the Holy Spirit. Oil is usually symbolic of the Holy Spirit. Being anointed with oil is representative of His power being poured out upon us for divine service. A little farther in this chapter we will discuss the role of the Holy Spirit in the process of holiness. Something that bears mentioning is that the priests spent seven days in the consecration process. Exodus states that: *"seven days shalt thou consecrate them."* EXODUS 29:35 The message beneath the surface is that it takes time to sanctify oneself. It is never an overnight experience.

Today, most people believe that holiness is an instantaneous achievement. We even preach it like somehow we make a decision to live for God, and that's all there is to it. The truth of the matter is that holiness is not an instant achievement; it's a never-ending process. Anybody that has attained any level of holy living testifies that it is a daily experience. You don't become holy in the blink of an eye. We are to constantly become more like Christ on a daily basis. It's a process. The scripture says, *"But we all, with open face beholding as in a glass the glory of the Lord, are changed into the same image from glory to glory, even as by the Spirit of the Lord."* 2 CORINTHIANS 3:18

Notice the writer says that we are changed into the image of God "from glory to glory." We actually progress from one level to the next. One of the most hypocritical people in the Body of Christ is the person that would make others feel as though they have no personal struggles. If you overcame a certain area yesterday, there is another area to overcome today. You can never consider yourself as having arrived because the standard is not your neighbor or some religious leader; the standard is Christ. Until you can say that your life is an exact replica of Christ, you have work to do.

The False Idea That Leaders Are Flawless Has Been a Major Issue with How We've Viewed Our Spiritual Leaders.

You would be surprised to discover how many people actually believe that their pastors are without any struggle or flaw. The sadder reality is that our pastors feed into these false profiles of sinless piety. Many pastors project that they don't have personal challenges. This is unfortunate, because one of the most powerful tools of any minister is transparency. A paraphrased version of an African proverb states, *"If you conceal your disease, it cannot be healed."*

The common mistake we make is to measure ourselves by ourselves. We tend to look at how we measure up to one another. The issue with this particular practice is that none of us is the true standard. For any of us to measure ourselves by another is to use an imperfect gauge. Jesus Christ is the only true standard.

One of the Greatest Causes of Faltering in the Pursuit of Holiness Is When We Miss the Mark and Give Up on the Process.

Experience proves that the commitment to the holy lifestyle does not mean that you will always reach the mark. The road to holiness is paved with hurdles. In the Olympics, the hurdle race involves much stumbling and tripping, but the runners continue the race until it's finished. You are not disqualified because you fall. Just keep running.

Sometimes the Believer Falls and Misses the Mark.

One of my biggest challenges was to come to terms with my frequent failure to meet the standards of God's word. Sometimes I would get close, but not exactly make it. In my heart I really believed that God would condemn me to Hell for not reaching the exact mark. I thought it was all or nothing. It took years of studying the Word of God to understand better. My father had talked to me about the grace of God but I really didn't comprehend it fully. Religion had so infiltrated my consciousness that I couldn't grasp the revelation of God's grace. The word of God never condemns us to Hell because we fall short. The word says in Proverbs: *"For a just man falleth seven times, and riseth up again: but the wicked shall fall into mischief."* PROVERBS 24:16

It's important to notice that there are two individuals mentioned in this text: a just man and a wicked man. You must see this; it is vital to the foundation of your understanding of holiness. The difference between the just man and the wicked man in this text is very significant in securing a revelation of holiness. The term *just* speaks of *a righteous man or one justified and acquitted by God.* The term *wicked* in Hebrew is: *rasha`*. It speaks of *one found guilty of a crime.*

The term *just* can be substituted with *saved,* and the term *wicked* can be substituted with the term *lost.*

The Only Difference Between a Saved Man And a Lost Man Is That the Saved Man Was Acquitted While the Lost Man Is Yet Marked Guilty.

The emergence of courtroom shows have taught all of us that a person can actually be guilty, and yet be acquitted, exonerated, or pardoned. Whatever the seated authority declares is final. This is exactly how we were saved. It was not because we were actually innocent. We were actually guilty, but Jesus pardoned us.

We are not saved because we were better than those who are not. We are saved because we simply accepted the sin-pardoning grace of God; it covered the evidence and set us free.

This is why the Apostle Paul said, *"And you hath he quickened, who were dead in trespasses and sins; Wherein in time past ye walked according to the course of this world, according to the prince of the power of the air, the spirit that now worketh in the children of disobedience: Among whom also we all had our conversation in times past in the lusts of our flesh, fulfilling the desires of the flesh and of the mind; and were by nature the children of wrath, even as others. But God, who is rich in mercy, for his great love wherewith he loved us, Even when we were dead in sins, hath quickened us together with Christ, (by grace ye are saved."* EPHESIANS 2:1–5

It was the love of God that covered up the evidence. The writer of 1 Peter 4:8 says that *"love covers a multitude of sins."*

God covered the evidence of our sin and guilt with the blood of his own son, and proceeded to offer His son as the guilty party in our place. He allowed Him to be found guilty on Calvary and canceled the debt with the sacrificing of His own son's blood.

When we come into the courtroom of justice, we simply step into the finished work of Christ. We come in boldly, because you can't convict a person for a crime that another man died for already. It is finished!

Think about this: What if you were guilty of a crime and all of the evidence pointed to you? What if you were convicted and sentenced to the death penalty, and someone stepped in and made himself to look just like you, and took your place? Suppose they died in the electric chair for you. Imagine they rose from the dead and simply asked in return that you would simply live a better life. Do you think that experience would have an effect on you? Sure it would! You would feel indebted to the individual that died. Your conscience would demand a certain response for such a self-sacrificing act.

Just as there would be a difference in the conscience of a guilty man pardoned, there is also an inner transformation in the heart of a person that has truly experienced the pardoning grace of God.

Whenever a Person Experiences a Real Conversion, It Is Always Followed by a Desire to Live for God.

I believe that the true mark of really being saved is displayed in a person's inner desire to live for God. If you say that you are saved and don't have a desire to please God, there is a serious problem. **If you have really been converted, you will have an overwhelming pull towards godliness even if you don't know how to accomplish it.** It's impossible to have a revelation of how He died for you, without acquiring a burning desire to live for Him.

The Bible says in ROMANS 6:4–6: *"Therefore we are buried with him by baptism into death: that like as Christ was raised up from the dead by the glory of the Father, even so we also should walk in newness of life. For if we have been planted together in the likeness of his death, we shall be also in the likeness of his resurrection: Knowing this, that our old man is crucified with him, that the body of sin might be destroyed, that henceforth we should not serve sin."*

The main message of this text is that once we know that Jesus died for us, we are spiritually and emotionally tied to His suffering. We become indebted because of His death. When we enjoy the privilege of being the sons of God, not by any deeds of our own, this reality delivers us from being willing participants in sin.

It Is the Birth of Unwillingness to Submit to Sin That Becomes the Basis for Holy Living.

As the word of God says: *"For the love of Christ constrains us; because we thus judge, that if one died for all, then were all dead: And that he died for all, that they which live should not henceforth live unto themselves, but unto him which died for them, and rose again."* 2 CORINTHIANS 5:14–15

The Individual That Is Deemed Holy in the Eyes of God Is Not Always Perfect In Deeds; But, He Is Always Perfect in Original Intent.

The holy individual always intends on doing right. They start out intending to honor God's standard. When they miss the mark they get up and start over again. The Bible says: *"For a just man falls seven times, and rises up again: but the wicked shall fall into mischief."* PROVERBS 24:16

Notice the just man errs as well as the wicked. Those committed to holy living miss the mark frequently, as do the lost, but there is a major difference. **When the just man falls, there is the inner government of his heart. This inner government does not allow a just man (*saved man*) to be spiritually calloused or desensitized to the will of God.** God makes the saved individual aware of his sin by way of his conscience.

Notice what the scripture says: *"How much more shall the blood of Christ, who through the eternal Spirit offered himself without spot to God, purge your conscience from dead works to serve the living God?"* HEBREWS 9:14

The term *purge* is the Greek word *katharizo*. It means to cleanse, to purge, or purify. The conscience of the child of God is constantly being purified. When the enemy attempts to focus our attention on anything contrary to the will of God, the Holy Spirit brings us through a spiritual catharsis. Our conscience immediately becomes grieved when we veer away from the will of God. This is one of the marks of genuine salvation. When a person is really saved, they cannot wander too far from God's will without being arrested by the Holy Spirit.

A Saved Man May Fall Down but He Can't Stay There.

Notice how PROVERBS 24:16 states that *a just man will fall seven times and get back up again.* Why? The just man gets back up because he knows that he is not condemned.

Jesus paid it all, and there is a holy consciousness resident within him; consequently, he can't camp out in sin. There is a new nature in him that constantly calls him to the higher call of God. The word of God puts it this way in 2 PETER 1:3–4: *"According as his divine power hath given unto us all things that pertain unto life and godliness, through the knowledge of him that hath called us to glory and virtue: Whereby are given unto us exceeding great and precious promises: that by these ye might be partakers of the divine nature, having escaped the corruption that is in the world through lust."*

This divine nature is placed within us to overcome our sin nature. When we do fall away, we have a higher nature drawing us back into the will of God. The term partakers speaks of a merger of the recreated spirit of a man with the Holy Spirit. God gives us the gift of the Holy Spirit that He might impart His nature to us and we might escape our own carnal weaknesses. He gives us His power to overcome our weaknesses.

As the word of God says: *"For I know that in me (that is, in my flesh,) dwelleth no good thing: for to will is present with me; but how to perform that which is good I find not. For the good that I would I do not: but the evil which I would not, that I do. Now if I do that I would not, it is no more I that do it, but sin that dwelleth in me. I find then a law, that, when I would do good, evil is present with me. For I delight in the law of God after the inward man: But I see another law in my members, warring against the law of my mind, and bringing me into captivity to the law of sin which is in my members. O wretched man that I am! who shall deliver me from the body of this death? I thank God through Jesus Christ our Lord. So then with the mind I myself serve the law of God; but with the flesh the law of sin.* ROMANS 7:18–25

Notice the writer talks about two laws: "The law of sin" and "the law of God." **"The law of sin"** is resident within every human being. Saved men have the "law of sin" in them as well as lost men.

I remember some years ago I was preparing my message one Saturday night for Sunday morning worship. I was in my Bible and I had the television tuned in to Christian television. I was basking in the glory of God's presence and the law of God was growing in me. I made one mistake: I turned the television station to a secular station. This particular station had a show entitled "G String Divas." To be bluntly honest, it was a show about female strippers. Instantly my flesh was awakened and another law took over. It was the "law of sin." Just that quickly I shifted from the spirit to the flesh. It actually took me a minute to gather myself and cut that stuff off and get back into the spirit.

Law of sin defined: *The law of sin is the pull of the flesh nature to go in the opposite direction of God's will.*

As we mentioned earlier, we are naturally born with the "law of sin" operating in us. We inherited the law of sin, in our flesh, from the first man, Adam. The word of God says, *"For as by one man's disobedience many were made sinners."* ROMANS 5:19

In ROMANS 7, Paul also mentioned the "Law of God."

Law of God defined: *The law of God is the upward pull of the Holy Spirit through the born-again spirit to reach for the holiness of God.*

The "law of God" can also be defined as the law of holiness. It is the very thing that created the conflict in Paul when he said he wanted to do right but didn't know how. That desire to do well was the law of God at work. The "law of God" creates a holy desire that is unusual to the natural man.

All Men Have the Law of Sin Operating In Them, but Only the Children of God Have the Law of God In Them.

An unsaved man has nothing to resist the pull of sin with. There is no law resident within him but the law of sin. There is only one nature in him. The saved man has a new law called the "law of God." It counteracts the pressure of sin.

Think of two balloons, one filled with natural human breath and the other with helium. Allow the naturally inflated balloon to drop and it will fall, helplessly, to the ground and lie there. If we let go of the helium-inflated balloon it will rise. The naturally inflated balloon symbolizes man under the "law of sin"; the helium-inflated balloon symbolizes man operating under the supernatural ability of the "law of God." Every time the helium balloon is released it rises. The question is why? The helium balloon is operating with a power that causes it to rise above natural limitations.

Likewise, the "law of God" operates from within the child of God and creates supernatural ability.

Every Time the Child of God Falls, the Supernatural
Power of God Causes the Individual to
Rise Above the Natural Limits.

The "law of God" will always work to restore the child of God back to the upright position. We are predestined by God to glorify Him in our living and He participates in our lives to assure success.

The word of God makes a powerful statement. It says, *"For we are his workmanship, created in Christ Jesus unto good works, which God hath before ordained that we should walk in them."* EPHESIANS 2:10

God created us to perform the good works of holy living. We were created to demonstrate the nature of our father, but there are some clear and essential steps necessary to allow the process of holiness to take effect. There are some fundamental keys that enable the holiness process to work in our lives.

SUMMARY OF CHAPTER FIVE

1. The Old Testament priest had a consecration process.
2. We also have a sanctification process.
3. Our sanctification should be visible to all to witnesses.
4. Holiness is a lifelong pursuit.
5. The pursuit of holiness is marked with falling down and getting back up again.
6. A saved man falls down but he gets up again.
7. The realization of Christ's death for us demands that we live for God.
8. God works through the conscience of a saved person.
9. There are two laws working in God's children: the law of sin and the law of God.
10. The law of sin is the pull of the flesh towards sin, and the law of God is the influence of the Holy Spirit towards holiness.

CHAPTER 6

FOUR KEYS TO THE HOLINESS PROCESS

There are certain things that one must have a firm understanding of to live a consistent life of consecration. With any great undertaking, there are principles and or keys to the process. Holiness is no different. There are certain factors that must be in place to succeed at such a noble and righteous aim.

Many years ago when I was in pursuit of a golf game, I had great troubles with even getting the ball off of the ground. I would have been ecstatic to simply see the ball take flight. I went to the range regularly with the most sincere intentions, and always left defeated and disappointed. One day, an older gentleman, who was a deacon of mine at the time, encouraged me to employ certain techniques or keys to driving the golf ball. He gave me some keys to a successful drive. As I employed his keys I noticed that I started to see some "relative" success.

Keys Are Designed to Give Access to New Territory.
Holiness Has Certain Keys.

Likewise, the process of holiness calls for the recognition and embrace of certain mandatory factors to see any real success. In this chapter we will explore some of these keys to success.

KEYS TO SUCCESS

1. The Holy Spirit Is the Primary Agent in the Process of Holiness.

The Bible says in HEBREWS 9:14: *"How much more shall the blood of Christ, who through the eternal Spirit offered himself without spot to God, purge your conscience from dead works to serve the living God."*

Notice that Jesus lived the spotless and sinless life by the Holy Spirit. Contrary to popular opinion, the Holy Spirit is for more than feeling good, speaking in tongues, and spiritual gifts.

The Holy Spirit First Impacts the Character of the Believer.

His main purpose is to empower us to live Godly and holy lives. The Holy Spirit is our immediate partner in defeating the flesh nature and executing the "law of God" (Living according to the spirit over the flesh).

The theological terminology for the Holy Spirit's work in our lives is sanctification. He sanctifies the child of God. *Sanctification is a gradual process in the Christian experience administered by the Holy Spirit to adjust our behavior.*

R. C. Sproul states that *"sanctification is a synergistic work."* Synergistic simply means that it requires the cooperation of at least two parties to succeed. In this process the two would be the Holy Spirit and us. We must submit to and cooperate with the Holy Spirit to actualize sanctification.

As the word of God says: *"Wherefore be ye not unwise, but understanding what the will of the Lord is. And be not drunk with wine, wherein is excess; but be filled with the Spirit."* EPHESIANS 5:17–18

One of the Most Misunderstood Benefits of the Christian Experience Is the "In-Filling" of the Holy Spirit.

People have misrepresented the Holy Spirit. They have portrayed Him as being weird, out of order, and forcefully dominating the personal will of individuals. As a result of this misrepresentation, many shy away from the very thought of embracing anything concerning the Holy Spirit.

The In-Filling of the Holy Spirit Is Unequivocally Essential to the Believer's Capacity to Live a Holy Life.

The power to live holy must never be perceived as one's own vitality; it is absolutely the enablement of God. When we submit to the in-filling of the Spirit, we welcome that divine enablement to completely take control of our lives. The in-filling brings the power of God to the life of the child of God.

The word of God states in ACTS 1:8: *"But ye shall receive power, after that the Holy Ghost is come upon you: and ye shall be witnesses unto me both in Jerusalem, and in all Judaea, and in Samaria, and unto the uttermost part of the earth."*

The power spoken of in this text is activated when the child of God is in-filled by the Holy Spirit. The in-filling is nothing really complicated or difficult to understand. To help grasp it, we'll use two illustrations. *At the first thought of the word "filling" one might think of a glass being filled with water. This sounds good, but there are some weaknesses in this particular illustration.* **A glass filled with water is inactive and has no bearing on anything outside of the glass itself.**

A better illustration might be that of a sailboat on a lake. As long as the sailboat sits on the lake, without the assistance of the wind, it makes no real progress. When the wind begins to blow and fills the sail, the boat begins to rapidly move in the direction of the wind. This is a very good comparison of how the Holy Spirit impacts our lives when we are filled. When we open up and surrender to His power, He begins to supernaturally carry us in the direction of God's will.

To Be Filled Simply Means to Be Controlled
by the Holy Spirit.

He controls us when we invite Him to take control of our lives. We must invite Him, because He will not force himself in.

The Holy Spirit is the gift of Christ to the church. His agenda is to assist us in glorifying Christ. **The greatest glory that we can bring to Christ is to reproduce His character and nature in our lives.**

The Bible says: *"But if the Spirit of him that raised up Jesus from the dead dwell in you, he that raised up Christ from the dead shall also quicken your mortal bodies by his Spirit that dwelleth in you. Therefore, brethren, we are debtors, not to the flesh, to live after the flesh. For if ye live after the flesh, ye shall die: but if ye through the Spirit do mortify the deeds of the body, ye shall live."* ROMANS 8:11–13

The emphasis of this text is, when we appreciate and submit to the Holy Spirit, we mortify or confuse the flesh nature, thereby neutralizing it. The more we neutralize the flesh and yield to the Holy Spirit, the more He injects the nature of God into the process.

As 2 PETER 1:3–4 says: *"According as his divine power hath given unto us all things that pertain unto life and godliness, through the knowledge of him that hath called us to glory and virtue: Whereby are given unto us exceeding great and precious promises: that by these ye might be partakers of the divine nature, having escaped the corruption that is in the world through lust."*

Notice the text says, he has "given unto us all things that pertain unto life and Godliness." Everything we need to live for God is within us. The main asset we have to empower the divine nature in us is the Holy Spirit. **His main purpose in our lives is revealed in his very name. He is called the "Holy" Spirit. His number one agenda is to produce holiness!** He comes to produce the holy nature of God in the lives of God's children. His main purpose is not to generate prophecy or healing; His chief cause is to assist us in duplicating the character of Christ to a dark and lost world.

The Holy Spirit Produces the Anointing.

The word of God declares in 2 CORINTHIANS 5:17: *"Therefore if any man be in Christ, he is a new creature: old things are passed away; behold, all things are become new."*

Notice the text says, *"If any man be in Christ."* The term *Christ* translates as *anointed one and his anointing.* In other words, the anointing makes one new. The anointing is synonymous with the Holy Spirit. When we are in the anointing, our "natural nature" is covered with his "supernatural nature" and this gives us supernatural ability. This supernatural ability makes all things new. We experience a new way of thinking and behaving as a result of the anointing.

When we merge our will with the anointed one, Christ becomes the new president of our lives. When we willingly make Him the new president of our lives, He lends to us all of His power and resources. He fully takes over our lives.

The In-Filling of the Holy Spirit Is like a Corporate Merger between Your Born-Again Spirit and the Holy Spirit.

In a merger, boards are redesigned and restructured. The authority is usually shifted to the people with the most interest. Ordinarily, a new person who understands and is committed to the new direction the company desires to go in replaces a former person.

The company in this scenario would be your life after conversion. The old president is the flesh nature. The new president is Christ, with the Holy Spirit as the chairman of the board. The Holy Spirit enforces the new agenda of Christ in the believer's life.

The word of God puts it this way: *"Howbeit when he, the Spirit of truth, is come, he will guide you into all truth: for he shall not speak of himself; but whatsoever he shall hear, that shall he speak: and he will shew you things to come. He shall glorify me: for he shall receive of mine, and shall shew it unto you."* JOHN 16:13–14

The Holy Spirit Is Working Constantly to Lead Us into Truth.

The Holy Spirit does His work in the boardroom of the mind. He impresses the will of God upon our conscience by coming against old thought systems and desires. The new president of your life, Christ, has His own way of operating, and He provides His own policy and procedure manual (the Holy Bible). The new manual overrules all of the past policies that the flesh and Satan have concocted together.

The writer of Hebrews says, *"For the word of God is quick, and powerful, and sharper than any two-edged sword, piercing even to the dividing asunder of soul and spirit, and of the joints and marrow, and is a discerner of the thoughts and intents of the heart."* HEBREWS 4:12

Notice, in this passage, the Word of God is called a discerner of thoughts. The Holy Spirit uses the Word of God to direct the decision-making process and thoughts of the child of God. The reason the Spirit uses the Word is because it contains the mind of God. He uses the Word to purge the conscience of the child of God. This brings us to the second key in the process.

2. The Word of God Is the Second Key to Holy Living.

There's a common saying: *"We are what we eat."* Any person that aspires to live a holy life must submit to a constant diet of God's word. As we embrace God's word, it builds up the inner man. The inner man has to be strengthened to fight off the flesh nature. This can only happen when we live in God's word. I mean we must become obsessed with the Word day and night. PSALMS 119:130 states, *"The entrance of thy words giveth light; it giveth understanding unto the simple."*

The Word is vital in the process of holy living. A person does not go into a dark room and wish that the darkness would go away. The only way to get the darkness out is to turn the light on.

The Word of God is the light. Before we come to Christ, our minds are filled with the darkness of the flesh nature. After we come to Christ, we have access to the light; but we have to choose to walk in the light or the darkness. It's up to us to flip the switch.

The word of God depicts this contrast between darkness and light in PROVERBS 4:18–19. It says, *"But the path of the just is as the shining light, that shineth more and more unto the perfect day. The way of the wicked is as darkness: they know not at what they stumble."*

God Has Provided the Guide of His Spirit and the Light of His Word to Keep Us on the Right Path; However, It's Up to Us to Walk in It.

If you never embrace the Word of God, you will never receive the full empowerment to come out of the bondage to sin. This is why a person can be saved and still has a mind filled with evil thoughts.

If You Don't Intentionally Turn the Light On, the Darkness Will Not Leave on Its Own.

As the Word of God is received, the nature of Christ is manifested in our being.

Another important observation concerning PSALM 119 is the term *entrance. If the Word never enters, it can't give the necessary light.* The entrance of the Word has a great deal to do with one's hearing. This entails not only hearing the Word, but how you hear the Word as well. A person can hear the Word academically and not attain the life-giving revelation of it that brings transformation. I have sat in many places where I heard the Word and never understood what I heard. Did it benefit me? No! **How one hears has much to do with the kind of ministry one is sitting under.**

There Are Two Primary Ways to Deliver the Word.
It Is Either Taught or It Is Preached.

Preaching is an exclamatory declaration of God's truth. Preaching usually appeals to the emotional side of a man's being. It is good and has a very real place in the plan of God. It is a primary avenue that God uses to prompt unsaved men to make a decision for Christ. God anoints the preacher to stir the emotion of an unsaved man to move towards salvation through Christ. Once the person moves towards Christ, the individual's spirit is then made alive.

The other primary form of hearing the Word is through the teaching ministry. This is the process of communicating information as well as understanding. Teaching is directed at the mental and spiritual faculties of the person.

The statement that I am about to make is not shared among all believers; however, **it is my opinion that after a person is saved, they need teaching.** We Preach People into the Church, but We Must Teach Them into the Kingdom of God.

The Kingdom of God is God's rule and government being manifested in the earth. Holiness is a Kingdom mindset that dominates the old dead flesh nature. One cannot enter into that kingdom mindset apart from teaching.

The only way to elevate behavior is through teaching. New behavior requires new information. People will do better when they are taught better. Even a saved person cannot live at a higher level than their understanding and understanding comes through teaching. This carries into the third key.

3. Recognize That You Cannot Live Holy in Your Own Ability.

I remember, as a young man, hearing people in the church declaring, "Holiness or Hell!" **The dreadful thought of Hell generated a false performance of holiness in most others and me.** When I say false holiness, I simply mean that we did the best we could to self-manufacture holiness. I tried to resist temptations in my flesh. Obviously this did not work. This is why the Holy Scriptures say, *"So then they that are in the flesh cannot please God."* ROMANS 8:8

The worst consequence of my attempts to live the life of holiness in my flesh was, when my flesh failed, I simply put on an act. I did enough to pass the people's test. This was dangerous, but, unfortunately, it is the state of most Christians today. When the flesh fails, they simply put on an act.

Most Christians Are Acting for the Crowd
Publicly and Struggling Privately.

At some point we were taught that holiness amounted to an extensive list of rules. The only thing most of us have heard about is what we should not do. Very few of us have heard much of anything concerning what we should do. There are specific moves that all believers must make if the lifestyle is going to permanently change. The scripture gives us some invaluable revelation to this process in JAMES 4:7. It says, *"Submit yourselves therefore to God. Resist the devil, and he will flee from you."* Pay attention to the order; the text says "submit to God" and then resist the devil.

You Cannot Resist the Devil Until You've
Submitted To God.

No believer will ever overcome the temptation of the flesh nature, apart from having totally submitted to God. To submit, in JAMES 4:7 simply means to personally place one's self under the influence of God. This has to happen willingly and not by force, or legalism, or religious constraint.

We Can't Live for God Before We Have Truly Made Him Lord of Our Lives.

When we make Him Lord, He will enforce every area of our lives with His own ability and power. Dr. Kenneth Ulmer once said, *"When He becomes your personal Lord, He'll also get into your personal business."* Your daily prayer must be that Christ would live in you and through you. You must willingly denounce Satan and the flesh nature and surrender your entire being into the hands of God. Once this truly takes place, Satan is brought low and his power is weakened. As long as you are attempting to live in the flesh you will always find it a struggle. When you get out of the flesh and transfer your focus to the ability of God, you will discover the power of God.

Holiness is Not Forced, It's Released.

True holiness is not something that has to be forced; it's released. It's the nature of Christ living in you and it comes out naturally. As the word of God says, *"Let your light so shine before men, that they may see your good works, and glorify your Father which is in heaven."* MATTHEW 5:16

The text speaks of letting "your light shine." It then proceeds to define what the light is. He says, "that men may see your good works." "Good works" is a reference to a holy lifestyle. The other thing the text clearly reveals is that we must *let* the light shine, not make it. The emphasis is on *let*. If we can let our light shine, it is safe to conclude that we can choose to not allow it to shine. It's a matter of personal volition or will.

Every Child of God Can Release the Light of Holiness or Restrain It.

It is when we learn to surrender to the ability of God to keep us that His power is activated in us. We release the light of holiness when we recognize that it is really Christ, and not us.

As the word of God declares in ROMANS 6:13: *"Neither yield ye your members as instruments of unrighteousness unto sin: but yield yourselves unto God, as those that are alive from the dead, and your members as instruments of righteousness unto God."*

The term *yield* in this text has a few meanings. It means *to place something beside or near, to place a person or thing at one's disposal, to bring to, bring near or to bring into fellowship.* In driver's terms, *to yield* means *to give in to another party.* The yielding party would follow the lead of the dominant party. When entering an interstate by way of a car, the person entering would have to yield to the traffic that is already in motion. The person entering cannot force their way into the traffic; but they must follow the lead of the other cars. If the driver attempts to force his way, there will always be an accident. If he yields properly, there will be a safe and natural merging.

If we are to walk in the light of holiness, we too must give in to the lead of the Holy Spirit. The Holy Spirit is always directing us into the things of God. We must stay in fellowship with the Spirit through prayer and worship, that we might be sensitive to His leading.
You Overcome the Flesh as You Surrender
to the Holy Spirit.

The word of God is replete with scriptural admonishment to rely on the power of the Holy Spirit to rise above the downward pull of the sinful flesh nature. For instance, ROMANS 8:5–6 emphatically declares: *"For they that are after the flesh do mind the things of the flesh; but they that are after the Spirit the things of the Spirit. For*

*to be carnally minded is death; but to be spiritually
minded is life and peace."*

The term *life* is the Greek word *zoe*; it is the *God
kind of life.* The highest form of *zoe* is to see the character
of God demonstrated in your lifestyle. Notice that the *zoe*
life comes as the result of being "spiritually minded."

To Rise Above the Restrictions of the Flesh Demands That We Fill Our Minds with Spiritual Things.

The former illustration of a balloon filled with
helium symbolizes the believer operating by the Spirit of
God. The other balloon filled with human breath
symbolizes the believer operating by the flesh. The
helium balloon always rose, while the natural balloon
always fell. As long as we attempt to live a life of holiness
in our flesh, it will never work.

The Bible states in PHILIPIANS 3:3: *"For we are the
circumcision, which worship God in the spirit, and rejoice
in Christ Jesus, and have no confidence in the flesh."*

This text clearly and directly states that we should
"have no confidence in our flesh."

My father, who is from a place called Woodville,
Mississippi, would often tell of his hunting experiences. He

told us of the characteristics of an animal called a possum. When the possum is being hunted, it will sometimes play like it's dead, until you turn your back, and then it gets away. This is very similar to the flesh, and why we must never put confidence in it. The flesh will only play dead for a while. Your flesh may be on the cross of crucifixion, but it is not dead. If you take your eyes off of it, it will attempt to get off of the cross. We must never trust the flesh. It only serves to distract our attention from the real source, which is the Holy Spirit.

A great problem that we have in the Body of Christ today is that many boast of how good they're living. The truth is, if we are living the holiness lifestyle, it is because God is keeping us.

Holiness Is a Work of Faith. It's Faith
in God's Ability in Us.

GALATIANS 2:20 says, "I am crucified with Christ: nevertheless I live; yet not I, but Christ liveth in me: and the life which I now live in the flesh, I live by the faith of the Son of God, who loved me, and gave himself for me."

Notice the writer says, "the life which I now live, I live by the faith of the Son of God." In other words, the life that is pleasing to God must be placed in the hands of God.

We Must Release Our Faith to Be Kept, Just like We Had
to Use Our Faith Initially to Be Saved.

It's all a work of God's grace through faith. We
must get out of the way and trust Him to manifest himself
in us. The Amplified Bible gives us a clearer view of
GALATIANS 2:20. It says: *"I have been crucified with
Christ [in Him I have shared His crucifixion]; it is no
longer I who live, but Christ (the messiah) lives in me; and
the life I now live in the body I live by faith in (by
adherence to and reliance on and complete trust in) the
Son of God, who loved me and gave Himself up for me."*

Pay very close attention to the three things the
amplified version brings out. It says we must adhere, rely,
and trust in Christ. When we do these three things, it
separates us from the limitations of our flesh and releases
His sovereign ability and power over our flesh.

4. Redefine Your Relationships.

To maintain a consistent lifestyle of holiness will
require some adjustments that amount to common sense.
Sometimes we focus so much on the deep spiritual
matters that we overlook the everyday common-sense
issues. A lifestyle of holiness will necessitate redefining
the way you live on a day-by-day basis. For instance,
sometimes we simply need to change the places we go

and the people we talk to. The wrong people in our lives are the greatest causes of flawed character.

You Can't Change Your Hang-Ups until
You Change Your Hangouts.

The Holy Scripture declares in 2 CORINTHIANS 6:14–15, *"Be ye not unequally yoked together with unbelievers: for what fellowship hath righteousness with unrighteousness? and what communion hath light with darkness? And what concord hath Christ with Belial? or what part hath he that believeth with an infidel?"*

The main idea of this text is separation.

A Major Issue for Christians Occurs When We Have to
Make a Choice to Divorce Ourselves
from Certain People.

Once you get saved, it's nearly impossible to run with the same crowd and go in a different direction. When your direction is east, you can't travel with people going west. Common sense! To live this life may call for a separation between you and any person that works against your commitment. This is sometimes hard, but remember it's mandatory to maintain your walk.

PSALM 1:1–3 says, "*Blessed is the man that walketh not in the counsel of the ungodly, nor standeth in the way of sinners, nor sitteth in the seat of the scornful. But his delight is in the law of the LORD; and in his law doth he meditate day and night. And he shall be like a tree planted by the rivers of water, that bringeth forth his fruit in his season; his leaf also shall not wither; and whatsoever he doeth shall prosper.*"

SUMMARY OF CHAPTER SIX

1. The Holy Spirit is essential to the believer's ability to live holy.
2. The Word of God exposes the light of God to our hearts.
3. A saved person needs teaching. We elevate behavior with information.
4. Holiness does not need to be forced. It's releasing the nature of God.
5. Holiness is a work of faith; it's faith in God's ability to keep us.
6. Holiness requires redefining certain relationships.

CHAPTER 7

HOLINESS AND THE "3D" LIFESTYLE

When I was a kid, I remember going to a 3D movie. They gave us special 3D glasses and explained that this particular movie experience would appear more vivid and real than any other we had ever seen. I thought that the announcer was just promoting, and I really did not anticipate very much. When the movie started, suddenly I became a believer. I became a 3D fan! The images seemed to leap off of the screen and right into my lap.

This little childhood experience of mine does not directly tie into the focus of this chapter; nonetheless, indirectly there is a powerful correlation. In the same way the 3D effect in the movie made the action on the screen leap into the hearts and lives of the movie patrons, there is also a spiritual process that causes the abstract concepts of holiness to spring into the real experiences of God's people. **In other words, this process causes holiness to become real and manifested in the child of God's lifestyle. I call it the 3D formula.**

You're probably wondering what this "3D" thing is. It is what I view as the three basic demands of consistent holy living. They are Desire, Discipline, and Dedication. Holiness is a definite process with specific responsibilities.

The Holiness Process Involves Having the Desire, Perfecting the Discipline, and Remaining Dedicated to the Process.

The Word of God says in 1 PETER 1:14–16: "*As obedient children, not fashioning yourselves according to the former lusts in your ignorance: But as he which hath called you is holy, so be ye holy in all manner of conversation; Because it is written, Be ye holy; for I am holy.*"

The term *be* literally translates as *become*. Once again this indicates a process. A major difference between salvation and holiness is that salvation comes without any work or effort on our part, no more than accepting Christ by faith. Holiness necessitates a personal effort; we work with God as He works with us.

We Must Co-Labor with God in the Enterprise of Personal Holiness.

Look at what 1 JOHN 1:7 says: "*But if we walk in the light, as he is in the light, we have fellowship one with another, and the blood of Jesus Christ his Son cleanseth us from all sin.*"

This term *cleanseth* is the Greek term *katharizo*. It is similar to our English word *catharses*, which means *to cleanse*. It literally speaks of being made free from the defilement of sin. Notice the blood cleanses us only after we walk in the light. When we commit our walk, He releases His power. The cleansing happens from the inside to the outside.

The three "D's" (desire, discipline, and dedication) are the very things that are necessary to walk in the light or to live a lifestyle that pleases God. We must desire to walk in the light. We must discipline ourselves to walk in the light. We must dedicate ourselves to this lifestyle. Let's explore these three elements a little closer.

THE "3D" FORMULA:

1. DESIRE

Desire is the engine behind any worthwhile undertaking. If there is no personal hunger, the motivation will always require external stimulation. **If you don't have a real desire, you will always need something or someone else to prod you.**

I remember some years ago I decided that I wanted to lose weight. I hired a personal trainer to help me. He would call in the mornings and wake me up. He would leave messages for me the night before. For a while his encouragement drove me to get up and exercise three times a week, but it did not last. I soon reverted back to my old ways and fired him.

As time went on, my doctor informed me that I had been diagnosed with type 2 diabetes. The doctor put me on the necessary medications and gave me a diet and exercise plan. I stuck to it consistently and I did not need anyone to call my house or stand over me in the gym.

Suddenly, I had something working in me that was greater than any external stimulant. I had the inner desire to change. This same power of desire plays into our ability to commit ourselves to holiness. We must tap into a real desire to please God in our lives.

Desire has to come first because God is not going to force us into holiness. God made man in His own image. **One of the main aspects of our makeup that qualifies us to be in God's image is that we have free moral agency. This means that we can choose to follow God or not. He won't impose His will upon us. We have the power of choice and we must desire Him.**

ISAIAH 1:19 says, *"If ye be willing and obedient, ye shall eat the good of the land."*

This text lays out a very necessary order for the child of God to understand. The text says that we must first "be willing" and then "obedient." God is not going to ever force us into obedience. It must always be an offering of the heart. Holiness has to be the desire of the child of God.

If you can recall, when God got ready to build the tabernacle, He instructed Moses to take an offering from all of those who had a willing heart. In other words, God was soliciting those who had a desire.

Our Desire to Live for God Becomes
Our Supreme Worship of Him.

The Bible says in ROMANS 12:1, "*I beseech you therefore, brethren, by the mercies of God, that ye present your bodies a living sacrifice, holy, acceptable unto God, which is your reasonable service.*"

This text is speaking of sacrificing the flesh nature and consecrating the body for holiness. The most important key in understanding this text is in the word *present.* **This indicates a personal desire and willingness to make an offering of one's self to God.** We must present our bodies willingly, out of personal desire and not by constraint.

The characteristic difference between a saved man

and a lost man is the direction of the will or desire. The Spirit of God produces in the heart of a saved person a desire to be like God and to please Him.

The Apostle Paul says in PHILIPIANS 2:13, *"For it is God which worketh in you both to will and to do of his good pleasure."*

Notice, God works in us the will to do his pleasure, or the desire to please Him.

The Desire to Please God Is the Foundation of Holy Living.

It was an amazing season in my life when I suddenly realized that I had developed a sincere desire to please God. I mean, I actually wanted to live for God. I never dreamed I would long to live right. I had been in church all of my life, but I had never experienced a deep inner desire to live for God. I was satisfied with just putting up a public front for people. I had been laden with guilt because of my inconsistent character. I really believed that everybody was in the same condition as me, and nobody could actually live holy. The thought never came to mind that it was possible to develop a sincere desire to live God's way.

This desire was birthed at a particular season in

my life when I had gotten very close to God through prayer and worship. I learned how wonderful it was to fellowship with God. Initially, I thought that this was a passing phase. Little did I realize that this experience would leave me a changed man. The more I worshiped, the closer I got to God, and the more my heart was purged. The fleshly desires that had controlled me all of my life began to lose their grip. I longed more and more for the things of God. My expressed love for God and His returned love to me generated into an increasing desire for God that became a passion.

The more we fall in love with God through worship and prayer, the more it creates a greater desire to please Him in our living. **Love creates desire and desire provokes behavior.**

Desire Comes as the Result of What We Truly Love.

When you love something, you desire it. I remember how committed I was to sin and the world. I actually loved living the way I was living. I would make time to indulge in my ungodly behavior. It was my love for sin that fueled a burning desire to continue in it. In the same way, our love for God will create an impassioned hunger to live for Him. When we really love God, we desire to please Him. Love and desire are inseparable.

JOHN 14:15 says, *"If ye love me, keep my commandments."* Notice how the text connects love and obedience.

Our Love for Him Creates Our Obedience.

Desire is so important because desire is the purest expression of the content of the heart. When God is really in your heart, there is an undeniable desire for Him.

When a person has a genuine salvation experience there is an automatic desire to want to live for God, and when the person misses the mark it grieves them. For instance, when the horrible persecutor of the Christian church, Saul, was saved on the Damascus road, there was an instant drive in him to please the master. He sought to know the will of the master.

The record is found in ACTS 9:1–6: *"And Saul, yet breathing out threatenings and slaughter against the disciples of the Lord, went unto the high priest, And desired of him letters to Damascus to the synagogues, that if he found any of this way, whether they were men or women, he might bring them bound unto Jerusalem. And as he journeyed, he came near Damascus: and suddenly there shined round about him a light from heaven: And he fell to the earth, and heard a voice*

saying unto him, Saul, Saul, why persecutest thou me?
And he said, Who art thou, Lord? And the Lord said, I
am Jesus whom thou persecutest: it is hard for thee to
kick against the pricks. And he trembling and
astonished said, Lord, what wilt thou have me to do?
And the Lord said unto him, Arise, and go into the city,
and it shall be told thee what thou must do."

2. DISCIPLINE

The second component in the 3D formula is
discipline. **The reason desire came first is because your
desires will determine your discipline.** If you don't have
steadfast desires, you will never increase discipline.
Discipline is practically synonymous with holiness. A
person of holiness is simply exercising discipline at its
highest level. Think about it; what is more difficult than
bringing discipline to the flesh nature? Nothing.

True Holiness Is an Exercise In Discipline.

Holy living demands discipline. **All of the biblical
characters that failed God were lacking certain
disciplines.** We must always remember that the flesh is
not saved and is vigorously and aggressively working
against the will of God.

Paul expressed it this way: *"But I keep under my*

body, and bring it into subjection: lest that by any means, when I have preached to others, I myself should be a castaway." 1 CORINTHIANS 9:27

Even though the text mentions the "body" specifically, it is in reference to the entire flesh nature. The phrase *keep under* means to *beat black and blue, to smite so as to cause bruises and livid spots like a boxer, one buffets his body, handles it roughly, discipline by hardships.* It literally means to take authority over your flesh by any means necessary. It speaks of coming to the place where you dictate to your flesh, and not your flesh to you.

The Bible says in 1 THESSALONIANS 4:3–4: *"For this is the will of God, even your sanctification, that ye should abstain from fornication: That every one of you should know how to possess his vessel in sanctification and honor;"*

The term "possess" literally speaks of owning and controlling your body. The mental picture is that of taking control of an untamed beast and domesticating it. We can only control this flesh nature to the extent we bring discipline to it.

Discipline is not a natural process. The flesh is most comfortable when it has no restraints or demands placed upon it. Consequently, discipline is the result of other factors that assist the individual's desire for a disciplined lifestyle. There are certain other factors that aid us in mastering discipline on any level.

Discipline Demands Vision.

The first thing that is mandatory to live a life of discipline is vision. A person must have a vision or a preview of a potentially greater future to master discipline. A fat person can bring discipline to their eating and exercise habits by catching a vision of a smaller and healthier body. It's the vision that aids the discipline. The text says: *"Where there is no vision, the people perish:"* PROVERBS 29:18

The emphasis of this text is this: "where there's no preview of a potentially greater future, the people, without vision, perish." The term *perish* literally translates as *cast off restraint.* **When there is no vision, a people have no sense of government, self-control, or discipline.** Where there is no vision, it is impossible to identify a purpose for living.

As we look at the culture across America, violence and crime are the result of a people that have no vision. There's no hope of a greater tomorrow. When there's no hope for tomorrow, there's no motivation for today.

What causes a medical student to endure the process and to discipline herself? She sees the light at the end of the tunnel. What causes a long-distance runner to keep putting one foot in front of the other, mile after mile? She has to have a vision of the finish line. **Wherever great discipline is found, it is always tied to vision.** A disciplined person sees where they can go and what can potentially happen if they endure.

When we can see the potential of tomorrow, it generates the necessary drive to constantly tighten the reins of our character and behavior today. If there's no real vision, we will always back out when the going gets tough.

Jesus was our example of this truth. In HEBREWS 12:2 it says, *"Looking unto Jesus the author and finisher of our faith; who for the joy that was set before him endured the cross, despising the shame, and is set down at the right hand of the throne of God."*

When we look at this text, it reveals a powerful truth. **Even Jesus had to have a vision to maintain His course.** The word says that, He was able to endure the discipline of Calvary and crucifixion because of the joy that was set before Him. He had the vision of His resurrection before Him. There must first be a vision before

there will be a constant and wholehearted discipline.
It Is Nearly Impossible to Get a Man
without a Vision to Develop Discipline.

Vision is even more significant in the process of producing the discipline of holiness. We will never be able to commit ourselves to the process until we get a very real preview of our potential.

When God began to really deal with me, I committed myself to living the way God wanted me to. There was one thing in particular that kept me on course. Even though I was committed in my heart to holiness, my flesh was still difficult to master. The thing that forever changed my life occurred when God revealed to me where He was going to bring me if I would maintain a committed life to Him. God showed me a great church that He would allow me to build. I saw a ministry that would be a haven for families. I also saw a ministry that would impact its community. He showed me a great television ministry that would reach millions. God even showed me books that would be written, by me, and read around the world. This great vision was directly linked to my daily discipline to live a certain way. If I wanted to see the vision, I had to perfect the discipline.

This created an interesting but very effective warfare in my mind. In one part of my mind I had temptations and desires to depart from the things of God. In the other part of my mind was the photograph of this great vision. These two impressions forced me to make a decision. Did I want to enjoy the pleasure of sin for a season and cancel my destiny, or did I want to push through the immediate gratification of sin and realize my full potential in God? I chose to hold my course and follow the vision. When your vision challenges your momentary desires, it's not a hard decision.

In the pursuit of holiness we must focus on the ultimate prize. We must set our focus on the vision before us. It is the vision that will counteract the pressure of the flesh and the pull of sin. The desire for the vision will always outweigh the pleasure of sin.

Discipline Demands Self-Assessment.

It's bad to think that you are what you're not, or to fool yourself into believing that you've arrived at a particular place of discipline before you've made it. Never fool yourself.

The Apostle Paul says in GALATIANS 6:3, *"For if a man think himself to be something, when he is nothing, he deceiveth himself."*

Genuine self-assessment is mandatory in the life of

a person that will develop any kind of discipline, especially the discipline of holiness. One of the great problems in the church today is that we spend too much time judging others while failing to assess our own character.

Jesus spoke against the spirit of judgment and encouraged self-assessment; He said, *"And why beholdest thou the mote that is in thy brother's eye, but considerest not the beam that is in thine own eye?"* MATTHEW 7:3

If there is no system of self-assessment we can tend to overlook flaws and fractures in our character that need attention. A disciplined person always has a self-assessment system to reveal the areas of concern. A part of this system is to ask the hard questions and to honestly analyze your thoughts and behavior. Many times we fail because we don't take an honest look at ourselves. Sometimes we're slipping long before we acknowledge it.

Disciplined People Are Always Constructively
Critical of Themselves.

The Bible says in 1 CORINTHIANS 11:31, *"For if we would judge ourselves, we should not be judged."*

There comes a time when we must all take a

detached look at ourselves and ask: "what am I doing? Is my behavior concurrent with my goals?" Do I like where I'm headed?" If the answer is yes, keep doing what you're doing. If the answer is no, you must make some essential adjustments in the way you do things.

What if King David had a self-assessment system when he first looked upon Bathsheba bathing? He might have never committed adultery and murder. Suppose Samson had a self-assessment process activated; chances are, he would not have lost his strength.

To Live a Lifestyle of Consistent Discipline
Requires Constant Self-Awareness.

When God was delivering me from a lifestyle of womanizing, I was confused about why I kept having setbacks. I did not want to live that way anymore, but I kept falling. One day the Holy Spirit caused me to do some self-evaluation. **When I took an honest look at some of the things I was doing and not doing, I realized that I was sabotaging the process.** I had not changed my phone numbers, consequently the people that I did not need to talk to could call me at will. I continued to frequent the same places, which aroused the same old emotions and desires. I was rebuking the devil and demons, when all the while I was my own worst problem.

The Bible describes this predicament in HAGGAI 1:6–7. It says: *"Ye have sown much, and bring in little; ye eat, but ye have not enough; ye drink, but ye are not filled with drink; ye clothe you, but there is none warm; and he that earneth wages earneth wages to put it into a bag with holes. Thus saith the LORD of hosts;* **Consider your ways."**

To live a life of holy discipline will require a constant consideration of the way you do things. Don't be the cause of your own demise.

Discipline Demands Authoritative Oversight.

The term discipline is indirectly related to the term *disciple*, but the process of discipline is inseparably linked to discipleship. To disciple is to teach certain disciplines by word and deed. This involves a proven and more mature individual overseeing the maturation process of a less mature person.

Proper Authority Provides a Visual Display of How to Behave.

It is this very process that makes education effective. As children, we learn the educational disciplines from older and more educated persons called teachers. They oversee our growth to insure proper development. Likewise, the spiritual development of holy discipline is also greatly dependent on those we are submitted to.

As the Word of God states: *"And he gave some, apostles; and some, prophets; and some, evangelists; and some, pastors and teachers; For the perfecting of the saints, for the work of the ministry, for the edifying of the body of Christ:"* EPHESIANS 4:11–12

The term "perfecting" implies a growing up. The truth of the text is that it takes a mature authority to watch over the development of spiritual discipline. This is accomplished in part because of the accountability factor.

HEBREWS 13:17 says: *"Obey them that have the rule over you, and submit yourselves: for they watch for your souls, as they that must give account, that they may do it with joy, and not with grief: for that is unprofitable for you."*

God sets certain authority in our lives for the purpose of accountability. Accountability simply speaks of having someone in your life that is going to hold you to the standard without compromise. In the pursuit of holy discipline, we all need someone to look over our shoulders to see if we're doing it right.

Accountability Is Vital in Maintaining Discipline.

Another thing authority does for us is to provide a visual example of how to live. When you consistently see someone living at a high level before you, it serves to refuel your passion. The process of holiness requires having someone modeling this lifestyle before you. Without that, you can be made to feel like you're the only one in the world. No one should submit to an unproven authority.

Never Submit to Someone Whose Life Is Not an Open Book. They Can't Develop in You What They Have Not Manifested in Themselves.

The Holy Bible says, *"Remember them which have the rule over you, who have spoken unto you the word of God: whose faith follow, considering the end of their conversation."* HEBREWS 13:7

Notice the writer says, *"follow their faith after you consider their conversation."* This means to look at their lifestyle. You should never follow undisciplined people.

1 CORINTHIANS 11:1 says: *"Be ye followers of me, even as I also am of Christ."* The term *follower* simply means to be an imitator. Paul encourages them to imitate

his lifestyle.

Every spiritual leader should be able to offer this challenge. Some disciplines are developed as we imitate those who serve as spiritual authorities over our lives. The right leadership will provide a visual display of a disciplined life.

Discipline Will Involve the Chastening of the Lord.

Remember, the entire holiness process is cooperation between the believer and God. God works to assist the child of God in the process. **A major part of developing the discipline of holiness is the chastening of the Lord.** It's not a very pleasant experience, but it is effective.

The Word says: *"Now no chastening for the present seemeth to be joyous, but grievous: nevertheless afterward it yieldeth the peaceable fruit of righteousness unto them which are exercised thereby."* HEBREWS 12:11

The term *chastening* is a synonym for discipline. In the Greek, it is the word *paideia.* It means *to correct mistakes and curb passions.* It also involves instruction, which aims at increasing virtue.

The writer reveals that the chastening or correcting

process is never momentarily rewarding. It does not feel good or pleasing while you're going through it, but it has tremendous benefits on our character. God will bring His children through a series of experiences and corrections to get us to where He wants us to be. The child of God cannot be out of line without God exercising tough love.

HEBREWS 12:6–7 says: *"For whom the Lord loveth he chasteneth, and scourgeth every son whom he receiveth. If ye endure chastening, God dealeth with you as with sons; for what son is he whom the father chasteneth not?"*

Sometimes when God is taking us through seasons of chastening it feels like we don't even belong to Him. The truth is that God chastens those that belong to Him. The reason we are even sensitive to the chastening of the Lord is because we belong to Him.

Discipline Is the Goal of Chastening.

In Hebrews, the writer goes on to reveal the after effects of enduring the chastening process. He says, *"it will yield the fruit of righteousness."* **The development of discipline produces righteous fruit. As we submit to the discipline of the Lord, it squeezes the nature of God out of us.**

3. DEDICATION

The third leg of this formula involves dedication. You will have to be dedicated to the process if you are to succeed. The whole idea about dedication to anything involves being committed to a singular focus. A person that is in real pursuit of holiness must have a committed focus in that direction.

James puts it in these terms: *"A double minded man is unstable in all his ways."* JAMES 1:8

If your mind is not singularly devoted to the attainment of the holiness lifestyle, the entire process is compromised. You must resolve in your mind that there is no other way. Holiness will require an unbending dedication.

Have you ever seen anyone who was on fire for God one week, and then the next week you could hardly find them? I once fit that description. I had zeal but I was not dedicated. I had a real fervor but I wasn't faithful. I was a strong starter but a poor finisher. I would make great declarations of what I was going to do, but when the pressure to follow through hit me, I frequently buckled. Holiness is not a fifty-yard dash, it's a marathon. You must be prepared to hold your course on a daily basis.

JOHN 8:31 states: *"Then said Jesus to those Jews which believed on him, If ye continue in my word, then are ye my disciples indeed;"*

Jesus is speaking of being dedicated to the daily process of the development of Godly character. We have many that start, but very few continue. It takes dedication to continue. Jesus said, *"if ye continue in my words then are ye my disciples."* Another term for "disciple" is disciplined one. A disciplined one is one who's fully committed and dedicated to the process. It's not enough to start; you must finish.

HEBREWS 12:1 says, *"Wherefore seeing we also are compassed about with so great a cloud of witnesses, let us lay aside every weight, and the sin which doth so easily beset us, and let us run with patience the race that is set before us."*

The writer of the text leaves the responsibility of identifying and eliminating hindrances up to us. He concludes this verse by saying that we must run this race with patience. Why?

The Process Is Slow and Sometimes Difficult, and If We Are Not Dedicated, We Will Ultimately Faint.

This is why Paul writes in GALATIANS 6:9, *"And let us not be weary in well doing: for in due season we shall reap, if we faint not."*

One of the biggest challenges of remaining dedicated to holy living is when we see ungodly people prospering in their sin. It can get hard to maintain your commitment to God's way when it looks like the people who are doing the same things you've turned from are living better than you.

The psalmist offers us a bit of consolation. He says, *"Rest in the LORD, and wait patiently for him: fret not thyself because of him who prospereth in his way, because of the man who bringeth wicked devices to pass. Cease from anger, and forsake wrath: fret not thyself in any wise to do evil. For evildoers shall be cut off: but those that wait upon the LORD, they shall inherit the earth."* PSALMS 37:7–9

SUMMARY OF CHAPTER SEVEN

1. Holiness will require three consistent qualities: desire, discipline and dedication.
2. Desire must come first, because God will never force us into the holiness lifestyle.
3. God views our desire to live for Him as worship.
4. Desire is generated out of love; what we love we will desire.
5. True holiness is a discipline experience.
6. Discipline requires a vision of the future potential.
7. Discipline demands self-assessment.
8. Discipline will require authoritative oversight in your life.
9. Proper authority provides accountability and an example of how to live.
10. Never submit to unproven leadership.
11. The pursuit of holiness will require an unbending dedication.

CHAPTER 8

THE POTTER'S PROCESS

There is an interesting process that goes into the development of pottery. I am in no way trying to suggest that I am gifted in this art, but a friend of mine enlightened me to the general procedure. As the various aspects of the potter's process unfolded, I saw a very clear relationship to the process of holiness that God institutes in our lives.

It is interesting that we find God instructing the prophet Jeremiah to go and observe a potter at work on his wheels. God intended to reshape the nation of Israel and He likened the process to the skillful actions of a potter.

The Bible says: *"The word which came to Jeremiah from the LORD, saying, Arise, and go down to the potter's house, and there I will cause thee to hear my words. Then I went down to the potter's house, and, behold, he wrought a work on the wheels. And the vessel that he made of clay was marred in the hand of the potter: so he made it again another vessel, as seemed good to the potter to make it. Then the word of the LORD came to*

me, saying, O house of Israel, cannot I do with you as this
potter? saith the LORD. Behold, as the clay is in the
potter's hand, so are ye in mine hand, O house of Israel."
JEREMIAH 18:1–6

This text deals with God preparing the Prophet
Jeremiah to bring a word of restoration to Israel (God's
chosen people). God wanted to inform them that He
would bring them through the process Himself. God would
take a hands-on approach to making them exactly what He
wanted them to be.

Holiness Is a Work of God in Our Lives;
He Forms Us by His Own Hand.

In JEREMIAH 18:1–6, God reveals some powerful
principles in a potter's house. As Jeremiah observed the
potter's process, he saw God's plan. The fundamentals of
this process are comparable to the New Testament
holiness process. **God is constantly molding us as a**
potter does his clay. When I was a kid, we sang a certain
song in church. It said, "please be patient with me, God is
not through with me yet." God is constantly molding us
towards perfection.

God's ultimate goal is to transform us into vessels
of honor. God does not want you and I to be common
vessels. A common vessel is reserved for common use. A

vessel of honor is reserved for the most noble of occupations.

The Bible says it a certain way in 2 TIMOTHY 2:19–21: *"Nevertheless the foundation of God standeth sure, having this seal, The Lord knoweth them that are his. And, Let every one that nameth the name of Christ depart from iniquity. But in a great house there are not only vessels of gold and of silver, but also of wood and of earth; and some to honour, and some to dishonour. If a man therefore purge himself from these, he shall be a vessel unto honour, sanctified, and meet for the master's use, and prepared unto every good work."*

The Purpose of Holiness Is to Make Us Vessels of Honor, Unto the Lord, and for His Work.

Holiness is a definite process and it is cleverly captured in the potter's process. **Just like the potter knows what he intends the vessel to look like at the end of the process, so does God have a predetermined image in mind for us.** God sees us as we will be at the end of the holiness process. He never sees us as we are.

Process Defined: Specific Activities Which Lead to a Predetermined Objective.

THERE ARE SEVEN BASIC
STEPS TO THE POTTER'S PROCESS:

Step 1. The Potter Digs the Clay from the Earth.

When a potter sees a muddy hillside, he sees vases, sculptures, and pottery. When we look at a hillside, we see dirt. The trained eye of a potter sees possibilities, potential, and value. This is comparable to God taking you and I from the soil of a sinful world while seeing our real potential at the same time.

ROMANS 5:8 says, *"But God commendeth his love toward us, in that, while we were yet sinners, Christ died for us."*

It does not matter what your condition is today, God has a purpose and plan for your life. Your life must be firmly placed in the hands of the supreme potter to realize your potential. God is the only one who knows how to materialize your potential. The fact that the potter takes the clay as it is, first points to a very important theological truth; **we are not holy before we come to God, we only become holy in his hands.**

The Prophet Isaiah wrote, *"Come now, and let us reason together, saith the LORD: though your sins be as scarlet, they shall be as white as snow; though they be red like crimson, they shall be as wool."* ISAIAH 1:18

Here is an invitation for sinful men to come to God in their current condition. Through the process of relationship, the Lord perfects the individual like a potter. The clay is nothing until it gets into the hands of the potter. **The only place of transformation is in the hands of the potter.**

There was a gentleman who went to a junkyard. He saw an old beat-up 1963 Mustang there. Everyone walked over this shell of a vehicle and viewed it as worthless. This particular gentleman bought the car immediately, without hesitation. He bought it for pennies on the dollar. He bought the car and took legal possession of the car. He even brought the car to his home. He took full ownership of the car. He did all of this while the vehicle was in deplorable shape. He accepted the car when others rejected it. He redeemed the car because he was skilled in restoration. He knew how to repair dings and dents. He also knew how to paint. He had everything necessary to restore it. The man accepted the car the way it was because he knew how he would do work on it later.

God Accepts Us as We Are, with Plans
to Renovate Us Later.

Step 2. The Potter Soaks the Clay in Water.

When a potter pulls the clay from the hillside it is hard and full of trash. The potter has to soak the clay to soften it. Soaking involves total saturation. The potter soaks the clay in water. *Water is a biblical symbol of God's Word.*

The Only Thing That Is Effective at Softening the Human Heart Is the Word of God.

The Word of God puts it this way: *"Now ye are clean through the word which I have spoken unto you."* JOHN 15:3

God saturates us in the word of God to soften our hardened hearts.

Sometimes We Use Means Other Than God's Word to Try to Change the Hearts of Men.

Many try condemnation to prepare the hearts of men for holiness. This is simply an attempt at using guilt to foster holiness. The wife who wants her husband to love God will attempt to make him feel bad. The pastor who wants his congregation to obey God might proceed to sentence them to damnation in every sermon; none of this works to soften the hearts of sinful men.

Another fruitless method of trying to effect change

in the human heart is self-righteousness. This involves trying to purify character by religious rituals and rules. You will soon discover that religious change is a temporary fix. The only thing that can soften the heart and cleanse the soul is the Word of God.

The Bible says in 2 TIMOTHY 3:16, *"All scripture is given by inspiration of God, and is profitable for doctrine, for reproof, for correction, for instruction in righteousness:"*

The term *reproof* is the Greek term *elegmos*. This word is found only in this particular text. It means *to produce conviction of a sinner, or to refute error.*

The Word of God Brings about
Conviction, Not Condemnation.

There were two men that had been bitten by a scorpion. Two paramedics arrived on the scene. One paramedic said to one of the men: "you should have known better than to get close to a scorpion. Scorpions are poisonous and will kill you." While this paramedic was informing the gentleman of his shortcomings, the man died, feeling bad about his actions.

The other paramedic, who found the other man, began to instruct the victim as to how to stay out of this type of situation. At the same time, this medic pulled out an antidote and administered it to him. While he instructed the man in better behavior, he gave him what he needed to recover. The man was restored and determined never to do the same thing again.

The first medic is what we call condemnation. It makes you feel bad about your error and watches you die. The second medic is comparable to conviction. It informs you of your error while it rescues you from your state.

Step 3. The Potter Slaps the Clay.

After the potter determines that the clay has soaked enough to soften, the potter begins to slap the clay. The purpose of slapping the clay is to force deeply embedded trash to the surface. If the trash is never removed, it will hinder the final product. The slapping comes across as a violent action but it is most necessary.

Slapping the Clay Is Symbolic of the
Chastening of the Lord in Our Lives.

The writer of HEBREWS states: *"For whom the lord loveth he chasteneth, and scourgeth every son whom he receiveth."* HEBREWS 12:6

The term *chasteneth* is the Greek term *paideuo*. It means *to educate or to discipline by punishment.*
God Chastens Us through the Word,
the Conscience, and Trials.

In the chastening process God exposes the hidden issues. This is uncomfortable because we don't care for being exposed. There's an old African proverb that states: "One cannot heal a disease that is concealed."

In The Holiness Process God Does Whatever Is Necessary to Get the Embedded Character Flaws Out.
Chastening Can Feel like Death.

Peter put it this way: *"But the God of all grace, who hath called us unto his eternal glory by Christ Jesus, after that ye have suffered a while, make you perfect, establish, strengthen, settle you."* 1 PETER 5:10

Sometimes God uses suffering and problems to purge our lives of things we need to eliminate. We would never extract these flaws apart from God forcing them out. Have you ever gone to church and the entire sermon dealt with your personal and private struggle? That was God whipping you into line and forcing some things out of you.

Step 4. The Potter Begins to Poke Holes in the Clay.

After the potter has gotten the clay purged of trash, he begins to poke fine holes in the clay. The purpose of this action is to eliminate air bubbles from the clay. If the air bubbles are not eliminated, it would compromise the future soundness of the product. Holes could develop and fractures could emerge. Eliminating the air bubbles ensures that the vessel will be solid through and through. This is representative of the Holy Spirit bringing conviction to the life of the believer. He gets rid of the things that would compromise the future product.

True holiness demands consistency through and through. We must not allow internal issues to compromise our ultimate potential. The Holy Spirit works to make us authentic from the inside to the outside.

The psalmist says: *"Behold, thou desirest truth in the inward parts: and in the hidden part thou shalt make me to know wisdom."* PSALMS 51:6

The air bubbles are not trash but they are things that can destroy the success of the process just the same. For instance, in our lives there are things that may not be considered as immoral but can still derail the plan of God for us.

Pride, Ego, and Selfishness Will Work to
Destroy the Character of God in Us.

The Holy Spirit pokes around until He eliminates all of these hidden issues.

Step 5. The Potter Centers the Clay On His Wheel and Begins to Mold It.

At this point the clay is pliable, moldable, and submissive to the potter's touch. As the potter takes the clay in his hand he begins to bring form to the clay. The clay begins to model the image that is in the potter's mind. This action is symbolic of the believer coming into the center of God's will. When we get there we begin to look like God's idea of us.

The Evidence of One Being Centered in God's Will Is When Your Will Dies and His Will for Your Life Begins to Dominate.

The text states in GALATIANS 2:20: "*I am crucified with Christ: nevertheless I live; yet not I, but Christ liveth in me:*"

Notice how the text declares that Christ lives in the believer. Once we get aligned with God's will, we die to our desires and He begins to live through us. **When we become sensitive to God's will, He begins the molding process.** As this happens, we transform into His desired image of us.

The Bible says in 2 CORINTHIANS 3:18, "*But we all, with open face beholding as in a glass the glory of the Lord, are changed into the same image from glory to glory, even as by the Spirit of the Lord.*"

The clearest evidence of being at this stage is repentance. **Repentance is not only being sorry, it involves having a very real change of mind and direction.** Repentance equals a willingness to turn to God's way.

The Apostle Paul said, "*Now I rejoice, not that ye were made sorry, but that ye sorrowed to repentance: for ye were made sorry after a godly manner, that ye might receive damage by us in nothing. For godly sorrow worketh repentance to salvation not to be repented of: but the sorrow of the world worketh death. For behold this selfsame thing, that ye sorrowed after a godly sort, what carefulness it wrought in you, yea, what clearing of yourselves, yea, what indignation, yea, what fear, yea, what vehement desire, yea, what zeal, yea, what revenge! In all things ye have approved yourselves to be clear in this matter.*" 2 CORINTHIANS 7:9–11

Notice how the writer makes a distinction between sorrow and repentance. This indicates that they are not the same thing.

Sorrow Produces Emotion While
Repentance Prompts Action.

Notice they didn't just feel sorry; they changed their course.

The Hebrew language uses two terms for repentance. One word is *Naham*—to feel sorry or to grieve to the extent of changing behavior. The other Hebrew word is *Shubh*—to turn back to God from sin.

The Greek language uses two terms. The first is *Metanoia*—to have another mind concerning one's sin. The second is *epistrepho*—to change position.

To repent, the child of God simply needs to acknowledge the sin for what it is. The child of God must call it like God calls it, and not try to dress it up or justify it. After you acknowledge your sin, ask God to forgive you. It's as simple as this. If you are sincere, God will forgive you instantly. Finally, you must ask the Holy Spirit to assist you in living in a new direction. Repentance is a change of living and we need the Holy Spirit to help us.

Step 6. The Potter Sits the Shaped Vessel upon a Shelf.

After the potter brings a desirable shape to the clay, he sets it upon a shelf. This action allows the vessel to dry and harden. This is representative of the isolation that often comes as a result of consecration. When you begin to model the image of Christ, the world will not welcome you too kindly. You will sometimes be distanced from old friends and family.

Paul writes to the young preacher Timothy and says, *"Yea, and all that will live godly in Christ Jesus shall suffer persecution."* 2 TIMOTHY 3:12

When your life begins to transform into the image of holiness, it will feel like you're in the world by yourself. Living for God is sometimes a lonely life. The road that goes in the way of God is traveled by few. The road that points to degradation is crowded. Be proud to be set on the lonely shelf of godliness.

Trials and rejection can make us feel as though it was all for naught, but there is a purpose. God is producing something in you through it all.

Find comfort in the sacred text which says, *"And not only so, but we glory in tribulations also: knowing that tribulation worketh patience;"* ROMANS 5:3

The hardening process produces patience and faith in God alone. When you're on the shelf you learn to rely on God. You learn to fellowship with Him. You become satisfied with Him alone.

Step 7. The Potter Puts the Vessel into an Oven for Preservation.

You would think that the shelving of the vessel is the final step. It's not. The potter takes the vessel off of the shelf and places it in an oven. This act is to preserve the vessel from cracking. **Putting the vessel through the fire prepares it for longevity.**

The fire conditions it to last. This is also symbolic of the work of the Holy Spirit in our sanctification. The Holy Spirit is the main agent in this process.

We Cannot Maintain Our Walk without the Aid of the Holy Spirit.

Jesus said, *"I indeed baptize you with water unto repentance: but he that cometh after me is mightier than I, whose shoes I am not worthy to bear: he shall baptize you with the Holy Ghost, and with fire:"*
MATTHEW 3:11

One of the main functions of fire is to purify. When I was a little boy, I would often get splinters in my hands from climbing trees and playing with wood.

Whenever I got a splinter in my hand or foot, my mother would get a sewing needle from her box. She would place the needle on the gas stove and burn the tip of it with the flames. I asked her why she did that, and she replied: "the fire purifies the needle and kills all of the germs."

The fire of the Holy Spirit enforces perpetual purification to the believer's consciousness. The believer's oven is the filling of the Holy Spirit. *To be filled simply means to relinquish control of your life and to allow the Holy Spirit to govern you.* It is His daily enforcement that keeps us pure from worldly defilement.

The Holy Spirit Anoints Us with the Fire of God and the Anointing Keeps Us in an Ungodly World.

SUMMARY OF CHAPTER EIGHT

1. Holiness is a work of God; He forms us by his own hand, like a potter.
2. The purpose of holiness is to make us vessels of honor unto the Lord.
3. There is a correlation between the Prophet Jeremiah's experience at the potter's house and God's process of holiness.
4. Just as a potter looks beyond the original condition of shapeless clay, the Lord also sees beyond where we are and focuses on what He can make of us.
5. The potter soaks the clay in water to soften it. The only thing that can soften our hearts is the Word of God.
6. The Potter eliminates embedded trash from the clay by slapping it; this is symbolic of the Lord's chastening in our lives.
7. The potter pokes holes in the clay to eliminate air bubbles. This ensures that the vessel will be solid through and through. This is representative of the Holy Spirit's conviction into the life of the believer.
8. The potter centers the prepared clay on his wheel for molding. This is symbolic of our being in the center of God's will for our lives and being fully compliant.
9. The potter sits the shaped vessel on a shelf to

harden. This is symbolic of God allowing us to experience isolation and separation as we harden into His image, without compromise.

10. The potter puts the vessel into an oven to bake. This is for preservation. This is symbolic of the fire of the Holy Spirit that preserves us in a sinful world.

11. We cannot maintain our walk without the Holy Spirit.

SECTION C

THE BENEFITS OF HOLINESS

R.C.BLAKES, JR.

CHAPTER 9

THE GREAT PRIVILEGE
OF HOLY LIVING

We miss out on so much when we fail to answer the call to holiness. **The enemy focuses our attention on the price of holiness because he doesn't want us to recognize the privilege.** When God called out to Moses through that burning bush on the backside of the mountain, it was not just a call to come up and to take off his shoes. It was also an invitation for Moses to embrace and meet with God in a way like no one had ever done before. It was a call to a more intimate relationship with God. GOD WAS INVITING MOSES INTO A POSITION OF PRIVILEGE.

The Bible describes it in PSALM 103:7, *"He made known his ways unto Moses, his acts unto the children of Israel."*

God was the God of all Israel but He had a different level of interaction between Himself and Moses than He had with anyone else. When God calls you to holiness it is an invitation to come into the secret place of the Almighty.

The Privilege of Holiness Is a Deeper Fellowship with God.

God reveals Himself in a more personal and profound manner to those that live for Him. God allows those who have sanctified themselves to find sanctuary in the Secret Place.

The scripture says, *"Follow peace with all men, and holiness, without which no man shall see the Lord:"* HEBREWS 12:14

When I first read Hebrews 12:14, I automatically assumed that the text was saying that without holiness a person would miss salvation. After digging into this text a little deeper, I got a better and more accurate perspective. The term "see" is not in reference to Heaven but rather it speaks of the measure of revelation one might qualify to receive. It speaks of being allowed to fellowship with God on an uncommon level. It's speaking of qualifying to experience an intimate fellowship with God. It means to show something or to allow something to be seen.

I remember hearing Bishop T. D. Jakes make a statement concerning intimacy: "Intimacy is simply the invitation of one to another that says: into-me-see."

Holiness Is A Stepladder into the Face of God.

ECCLESIASTES 12:13 says, "Let us hear the conclusion of the whole matter: Fear God, and keep his commandments: for this is the whole *duty* of man." Notice the term "duty" is italicized. When a word is italicized in the Bible it means that the word was not there in the original text. It was added to help make the transition from Hebrew to English. When we read the text without the addition of duty, it reads somewhat differently: *"keep his commandments: for this is the whole of man."* **Only obedience to God or holiness brings wholeness in life.** If a man desires to experience wholeness and fulfillment in life, he must perfectly align his endeavors with the will of God for his life.

A Person Is Never Fulfilled or Complete Apart
From Holiness; Holiness Creates Wholeness.

The main reason that holiness creates wholeness is because it unites us to the creator. We can never feel total or complete, apart from the intimate embrace of our Father. Even in the natural, grown people who have done well for themselves financially and otherwise, often search for their biological parents. If there has not been the embrace of a father or the love of a mother, they feel fractured without that embrace. How much more must we have the intimate interaction of our God? Holiness creates that climate.

The Bible makes a powerful statement. It says, *"holiness becometh thine house, O LORD, for ever."* PSALMS 93:5

God makes His sanctuary where holiness is established. When our lives are dedicated to the holiness of God, He abides with us in a way that is not experienced by most men.

When sin is dominating a person or even a church, the presence of God is very difficult to attract. God reveals Himself where He sees the beauty of His own reflection (holiness).

This is why the Bible admonishes, *"Wherefore come out from among them, and be ye separate, saith the Lord, and touch not the unclean thing; and I will receive you."* 2 CORINTHIANS 6:17

The term "receive" literally means *to welcome kindly and with favor.* The message of the text is that we must create space between ungodliness and ourselves. **We escape the evilness of the world through the very nature of God that dwells in us by the Holy Spirit.**

IMPERFECTLY HOLY

There Are Various Degrees of Intimacy
and Fellowship with God.

There's an interesting prophetic illustration
depicted in EZEKIEL 47:3–5. It states: *"And when the
man that had the line in his hand went forth eastward,
he measured a thousand cubits, and he brought me
through the waters; the waters were to the ankles.
Again he measured a thousand, and brought me
through the waters; the waters were to the knees. Again
he measured a thousand, and brought me through; the
waters were to the loins. Afterward he measured a
thousand; and it was a river that I could not pass over:
for the waters were risen, waters to swim in, a river that
could not be passed over."*

The "waters" are symbolic of fellowship in the Spirit.
Notice how the degrees move from ankle deep and go all
the way up to over the head. This is a wonderful depiction
of the many degrees of fellowship believers might
experience with God.

Most Have Only Embraced an Ankle-Deep Walk with
God, Never Fully Committing Beyond the Comfort Zone.

God is calling for you to get in over your head and
to get baptized in the very power of God.

Even in Jesus' relationships he demonstrated various degrees of intimacy. Jesus did certain things with the multitude, certain things He reserved for his twelve disciples, and ultimately He did special things with Peter, James, and John only.

A Part of the Blessing of Sanctification Is That It Affords Us a Greater Experience with God.

Jesus said on a certain occasion, "*Ye are my friends, if ye do whatsoever I command you. Henceforth I call you not servants; for the servant knoweth not what his lord doeth: but I have called you friends; for all things that I have heard of my Father I have made known unto you.*" JOHN 15:14–15

This is a powerful passage of scripture because Jesus reveals two different levels of relationship. One level is that of a servant, while the other is a friend. The text reveals the qualifications for friendship. He says, "do what I command." We enter into friendship with God as we follow His commands. People that walk in holiness definitely experience a closer walk with God.

The term "friends" unveils a powerful detail. In the fifteenth verse of John 15, Jesus says, "*I have not called you servants but friends; for servants know not what the Lord doeth.*" The emphasis of the text is that friendship generates a deeper level of sharing. Think about it; a con may spend months befriending a person before they strike. Why?

People share more with their friends. **Likewise, God shares more with His friends than He does with mere servants. Why? God trusts His friends. Can God trust you?** Friendship comes through obedience, and obedience produces a deeper revelation of God. Jesus said to them that He revealed all things to them and he called them friends.

God Reserves a Special Place for
Those Who Live for Him.

The scripture says in PSALM 24:3–4, *"Who shall ascend into the hill of the LORD? Or who shall stand in his holy place? He that hath clean hands, and a pure heart; who hath not lifted up his soul unto vanity, nor sworn deceitfully."*

This Psalm is in reference to the child of God that would dare to enter into the ultimate experience of God's *shek-kinah glory*, which is His manifested presence. In PSALM 24 the writer gives us a list of requirements to meet before we may experience an intimate walk with God. He mentions having "clean hands," which is symbolic of purifying the works of the flesh nature. It then goes on to talk about having a "pure heart," which points to the spirit being sensitive to the things of God. It then talks about not having the "soul lifted up in vanity." The soul is comparable to the mind being integrated to the thoughts of God. Finally, the text deals with "not swearing," which involves keeping the mouth under control.

These are the four areas that must be under divine control if we will qualify to enjoy the intimate presence of God. We must sanctify the deeds of our hands. We must judge the content and motivation of our hearts. We must be certain that our spirit man is keyed in on the will and voice of God. Finally, we must control our mouths that we don't grieve the Holy Spirit. **This deals with a total preparation of the whole being to receive the Holy presence of God. When this preparation is made, God allows the individual to walk where most men never go.**

The Bible says, *"And the very God of peace sanctify you wholly; and I pray God your whole spirit and soul and body be preserved blameless unto the coming of our Lord Jesus Christ."* 1 THESSALONIANS 5:23

Pay close attention to the word *"wholly."* It speaks of an unimpeded presentation of a person's entire being to God as an offering. The psalmist in PSALM 24 specifies the depth of fellowship and intimacy the child of God should yearn for with God.

It says, *"this is the generation of them that seek him, that seek thy face, O Jacob. Selah."* PSALMS 24:6

Note the text says this generation seeks the face of God. The indication is that there are other generations that sought something other than God's face. **What's the big deal with God's face?** His face represents His nature and character. **Holiness is the character of God rubbed off on the believer.** To seek His face is to seek His character and nature.

Most people only seek God's hand. His hand is symbolic of His benefits and gifts. **His hand represents His "presents." His face embodies His "presence."** Most generations have only sought God's hand (presents), while ignoring His face (presence). These generations of saints mostly desire a material manifestation of God.

The Word of God states in JOHN 6:25–26: *"And when they had found him on the other side of the sea, they said unto him, Rabbi, when camest thou hither? Jesus answered them and said, Verily, verily, I say unto you, Ye seek me, not because ye saw the miracles, but because ye did eat of the loaves, and were filled."*

We promote ministry on the premise of what God will do for us. God is searching for a people who will love Him just for who He is. God's searching for the people that are asking, "What can we do for God?" To seek His face involves knowing God intimately, but at the same time, it's being totally exposed before Him. This is why most people never endeavor to embrace God's face.

When We Get in Proximity of God's Face, Not Only Does He Expose Himself to Us, but We Are Exposed to Him as Well.

The Bible says in II CORINTHIANS 3:17–18, *"Now the Lord is that Spirit: and where the Spirit of the Lord is, there is liberty. But we all, with open face beholding as in a glass the glory of the Lord, are changed into the same image from glory to glory, even as by the Spirit of the Lord."*

Once we get into the glorious presence of God, He leaves us changed forever. A person cannot go into the presence of God and come out the same. When the presence of God is in a church, people don't leave the same. God's presence makes alterations in the people. **Holiness puts us in His face and His face creates transformation.**

God's Face Is Contagious; Once You
Get There, You Must Return.

There's a famous brand of potato chips whose slogan states that "you can't eat just one." I tried them, and it's true. This minutely reminds me of the precious presence of God. Once you are privileged to get into His face, you can't live without Him.

The psalmist says, *"As the hart panteth after the water brooks, so panteth my soul after thee, O God. My soul thirsteth for God, for the living God: when shall I come and appear before God?"* PSALM 42:1–2

When the deer is panting after the water brooks, it is often a matter of life or death. Sometimes the deer hides in the brook from predators, with just its nose exposed. Other times it is so parched that the brook is a necessity for sustenance. Once we get into the presence of God, it creates the same intensity of the deer's longing. It becomes a matter of life and death. We cannot climb into the presence of God and leave the same.

MATTHEW 17:2–9 states: *"And was transfigured before them: and his face did shine as the sun, and his raiment was white as the light. And, behold, there appeared unto them Moses and Elias talking with him. Then answered Peter, and said unto Jesus, Lord, it is good for us to be here: if thou wilt, let us make here three tabernacles; one for thee, and one for Moses, and one for Elias. While he yet spake, behold, a bright cloud overshadowed them: and behold a voice out of the cloud, which said, This is my beloved Son, in whom I am well pleased; hear ye him. And when the disciples heard it, they fell on their face, and were sore afraid. And Jesus came and touched them, and said, Arise, and be not afraid. And when they had lifted up their eyes, they saw no man, save Jesus only. And as they came down from the mountain, Jesus charged them, saying, Tell the vision to no man, until the Son of man be risen again from the dead."*

These selected disciples had the privilege of climbing straight into the presence of God and they didn't want to leave. The sad fact is that most Christians have never embraced God face-to-face. **There were three things that happened on this mountain of transfiguration: heavenly things were revealed clearly, God spoke directly to them, and God trusted them with secrets.**

When we live the holiness lifestyle, God begins to reveal things to us personally. There are too many believers depending on others to tell them what God is saying or doing. When you live in God's presence, He'll reveal His will and voice to you personally.

Holy Living Will Silence the Devil.

Satan is also known as an accuser of the brethren. He finds most of his time banking on our downfalls. He sets up temptation traps for us and broadcasts the fact that we won't last. This is what he did with Job.

JOB 1:6–11 states: *"Now there was a day when the sons of God came to present themselves before the LORD, and Satan came also among them. And the LORD said unto Satan, Whence comest thou? Then Satan answered the LORD, and said, From going to and fro in the earth, and from walking up and down in it. And the LORD said unto Satan, Hast thou considered my servant Job, that there is none like him in the earth, a perfect and an upright man, one that feareth God, and escheweth evil? Then Satan answered the LORD, and said, Doth Job fear God for nought? Hast not thou made an hedge about him, and about his house, and about all that he hath on every side? thou hast blessed the work of his hands, and his substance is increased in the land. But put forth thine hand now, and touch all that he hath, and he will curse thee to thy face."*

Notice how Satan prognosticated Job's fall. This is exactly what Satan does with us on a daily basis. He banks on our decline from God's will. We must view every temptation and challenge as an opportunity to silence the voice of the adversary. Just like Job withstood the temptation and glorified God, we too must glorify God through every testing, temptation, or challenge. Let us shut the devil's mouth. The enemy says that there are no Christians living the holiness lifestyle. The enemy declares that the church will be a pool of hypocrisy and the testimony of the Body of Christ will have no impact. When we make a stand for Godliness, we thwart the plans of the enemy. Let us answer the call of holiness and rise up as a mighty army in the earth. God is depending on us.

Holiness Will Cover the Nation with God's Blessings.

There is another great effect that the holiness of God's people will have upon the earth. **When God's people live for Him, it creates a divine fallout upon the nation. Holiness launches the blessings of God upon a whole nation.**

The popular text in 2 CHRONICLES states: *"If my people, which are called by my name, shall humble themselves, and pray, and seek my face, and turn from their wicked ways; then will I hear from heaven, and will forgive their sin, and will heal their land."* 2 CHRONICLES 7:14

God says when His people understand the responsibility to live for Him and meet His basic requirements, the result would be the healing of the land. The healing of the land speaks of God moving upon the landscape and rectifying the many ailments that the departure from God's way brings about.

For instance, holiness is the answer to sexually transmitted disease, holiness is the answer to corruption in government, and holiness is the answer to global hunger. When men live like God commands, the blessings of God take over.

DEUTERONOMY 28:1–3 says: "*And it shall come to pass, if thou shalt hearken diligently unto the voice of the LORD thy God, to observe and to do all his commandments which I command thee this day, that the LORD thy God will set thee on high above all nations of the earth: And all these blessings shall come on thee, and overtake thee, if thou shalt hearken unto the voice of the LORD thy God. Blessed shalt thou be in the city, and blessed shalt thou be in the field.*"

Holiness brings healing, restoration, family cohesiveness, financial overflow, and everything that is good and godly.

The Bible says in PROVERBS 14:34, "*Righteousness exalteth a nation: but sin is a reproach to any people.*"

Moral uprightness will cause a people to rise in every way, but sin condemns a nation to defeat and decay. The call of holiness is a call to intimacy with God. It's a call to prosperity. It's a call to national elevation. America needs the people of God to model God's standard for living. When God's people live God's way, the whole nation will be blessed.

The most profound blessing that our demonstration of holiness will have on the nation is that the unbeliever will be converted by the testimony of our lifestyles. When God's people live for Him, the spirit of evangelism sweeps a nation and becomes contagious.

Jesus puts it so eloquently in MATTHEW 5:14–16: "*Ye are the light of the world. A city that is set on an hill cannot be hid. Neither do men light a candle, and put it under a bushel, but on a candlestick; and it giveth light unto all that are in the house. Let your light so shine before men, that they may see your good works, and glorify your Father which is in heaven.*"

SUMMARY OF CHAPTER NINE

1. Holiness creates the groundwork for a deeper fellowship with God.
2. Holiness causes God to expose Himself to us in an uncommon fashion. God exposes Himself to you.
3. A person is never whole until they live for God. Holiness is wholeness.
4. Holiness puts us in God's face and His face creates transformation.
5. Holiness silences the enemy's voice.
6. Satan is planning on our failure to reflect on God and defuse our witness.
7. Holiness covers the entire nation with God's blessings.
8. Holiness creates an increase in effective evangelism; the world is drawn to Christ by our lifestyle.

R.C.BLAKES, JR.

CHAPTER 10

HOLINESS AND INTEGRITY

Holiness is a spiritual concept that is impossible for the world to understand. **When we live the holiness lifestyle, it is perceived as integrity to the world.** The people of God that live in accordance with His will are observed by the world as a people of integrity. Unfortunately, the idea of integrity today is an unfamiliar view. Even in the church we see the level of integrity waning. People don't have a word anymore. We have excelled in charisma, but we are lacking in character. We are more talented and gifted and less consecrated.

Integrity Defined: To Possess Soundness of Character and to Adhere to a Code of Values.

Have you noticed lately that the overall character of many "Christians" is often less stable than that of "unsaved people"? I believe that this is in direct relation to our departure from holiness. The culture of the church has changed. We are becoming less sacred and more politically correct. We have adopted the world's philosophies and have consequently suffered a moral fault. There has been a shaking of the foundations of

Christendom, and we have been found morally deficient.

When a People Departs from Holiness,
Their Basic Morality Suffers.

The Word of God says: "*Righteousness exalteth a nation: but sin is a reproach to any people.*" PROVERBS 14:34

I firmly believe that if we raise children in holiness it will have a direct impact on their values and overall integrity in life.

When my youngest daughter Rachel was a little girl, she asked me a powerful question. She asked, "Daddy, why do you teach about holiness so much?" I proceeded to explain to her that holiness is God's design for human living. I also told her that if people would live holy lives, we wouldn't have as many problems in the world as we do. She shook her head to confirm that she understood. I believe the standard of holiness will influence her way of thinking long after I'm in Heaven. Praise God!

When we live consecrated lives we are perceived as being a people of integrity, and this produces favor with God and mankind. Integrity brings favor on the job, in the neighborhood, and wherever else we might plant our feet. When you commit to live the holiness lifestyle, it will increase favor on your life.

The integrity of a person is really the end result of some other things at work; **your character is a combination of two basic factors, values and ethics.**

VALUES: Values Are Personal And Internal. Values Speak of What You Consider Valuable or Consider Significant.

Values determine how you judge matters in life. **Values change from one person to the next, depending on upbringing and exposure to truth.** A person brought up in a Christian home and under the Word of God should have a different set of values. Our values stem directly from what we believe and what we are exposed to. Values exist deep within the heart of an individual.

What You Value, You Fight For.

ETHICS: Ethics Are the Social Gauge of How One Should Interact with Other People. Ethics Are Social Rules.

What is ethical also changes from one social setting to the next. What is ethical in certain settings may be unethical in others. The ethics of a true Christian must always be based on God's way of doing things. The Christian's driving ethical rule is, "do unto others as you would have them do unto you." Of course, the world operates from a much different rulebook. The world has a different set of values. Ethical or non-ethical behavior is always tied to a person's value system. When a person can behave unethically in any given setting, it goes back to poor values. **A person that behaves ethically, even when they are not under scrutiny, has a strong set of values.** Unlike values, ethics are not buried within the heart of a person. Ethics will always show up in the behavior. A person with strong values and firm ethics will not take company inventory or more time for lunch than allowed. **Ethics are values in demonstration. Values and ethics lead to integrity.**

INTEGRITY: Integrity Is the Consistency between One's Values and Ethical Behavior.

If we listen to the word *integrity* itself, it tells its own story. The word *integrity* sounds much like a relative of the word integration. Integration means to combine or bring together. Though there is no connection between these words in terms of etymology, there is a significant connection in terms of practicality. **Integrity is the combination or bringing together of proper values and ethics.**

Integrity is the birth child of values and ethics being displayed in behavior.

A person of integrity knows what's right and does it without oversight. Integrity is the presence of an internal government. Integrity is the thing that keeps some people strong where others easily fall. What is the difference? If there is a weak value system, there is nothing to anchor the character of the person. They can know what is right and still do the opposite without remorse, because they lack internal government. There's nothing directing them from within.

The Bible says in PSALM 51:10, *"Create in me a clean heart, O God; and renew a right spirit within me."*

I love this text because the emphasis is on the heart. The writer is talking about creating a pure consciousness or thought system to govern his life.

One of the interesting things about a diamond is that one cannot determine the quality or integrity of a diamond by what is seen on the surface. There are stones that look beautiful to the naked eye but are severely flawed beneath the surface. Hidden flaws lessen the value of a stone. The real worth of the stone cannot be established until one takes a look with an instrument that reveals deeper than a surface view.

The Key to External Brilliance Is Internal Excellence.

A biblical term that describes one aspect of the character of a person with little to no integrity is the term *hypocrite.* The term *hypocrite* literally means to be an actor, pretender, or stage player. When there is a lack of integrity in a person's life they spend their time acting like they are what they're not. It has to be tiresome.

One passage says, *"A false balance is abomination to the LORD: but a just weight is his delight."* PROVERBS 11:1

There are people who have made a profession of creating an illusion around them. They appear one way externally, but their hearts are in another place. When I was a kid, there was a song that said: "Smiling faces sometimes tell lies." I have found as an adult that they lie most of the time.

True Integrity Cannot Be Determined by Anything Other Than What Kind of Person You Are Privately.

It is not enough to give an appearance of integrity and be corrupt in your heart. We can't take a political approach to life. In other words, we can't say one thing and do another. We must be determined to be genuine.

This is why the psalmist wrote, *"Behold, thou desirest truth in the inward parts: and in the hidden part thou shalt make me to know wisdom."* PSALM 51:6

God's not impressed with disguises. He wants authenticity through and through. People get caught up in trying to impress other people and fail to realize that the one that really matters is God. God is looking beyond our superficial masks. He looks at what is in the heart. PROVERBS 29:26 states: *"Many seek the ruler's favor; but every man's judgment cometh from the LORD."*

There Are Only Two Individuals That Know the True Level of Your Integrity and They Are You and God.

THREE REASONS TO LIVE A LIFE OF INTEGRITY:

1. You Have to Live with Yourself.

You have to face yourself every morning. The person in the bathroom mirror is the one you have to be pleased with. Are you genuinely happy with yourself? Are you proud of yourself? We often want other people to be proud of us, when the most important thing is to find pride in ourselves. There's nothing worse than self-disappointment. Joseph gives us an example of the importance of being able to respect yourself.

In GENESIS 39:7–9 it says: *"And it came to pass after these things, that his master's wife cast her eyes upon Joseph; and she said, Lie with me. But he refused, and said unto his master's wife, Behold, my master wotteth not what is with me in the house, and he hath committed all that he hath to my hand; There is none greater in this house than I; neither hath he kept back any thing from me but thee, because thou art his wife:* **how then can I do this great wickedness, and sin against God?***"*

Joseph's integrity was too important to him to relinquish it for a temporary thrill. There was too much at stake. He would have to deal with the guilt of his actions. He would have had to manage a false lifestyle. He would have had to reap what he had sown.

2. Somebody Is Watching Your Example.

Another very important reason to live a life of integrity is because you are always being observed by others. You don't just live for you alone. Someone is watching your example and will emulate your behavior.

The Bible says, *"Let us not therefore judge one another anymore: but judge this rather, that no man put a stumbling block or an occasion to fall in his brother's way."* ROMANS 14:13

You Would Be Amazed at How Many People Are
Following Your Lifestyle Step-by-Step.

One of the most dreadful situations would be to
meet God and find out that others went astray because of
my hypocrisy. On the other hand, what a joy it will be to
meet God and to find out that others lived better lives
because of my example of integrity.

3. You Will Reap What You Sow.

Our lives are a sowing field. Everything we do will
come back to us in multiplied form. If we live with
integrity and fairness, we will reap the same from life. I
am a firm believer that many people who suffer terrible
circumstances are simply reaping a crop they've sown. If
we live right, it will come back to us.

According to GALATIANS 6:7, it states, *"Be not
deceived; God is not mocked: for whatsoever a man
soweth, that shall he also reap."*

SUMMARY OF CHAPTER TEN

1. Holiness is a spiritual concept and is impossible
    for the world to comprehend. Our Holy living
    translates into integrity to the world.
2. A departure from holiness creates a lapse in
    overall morality.
3. Integrity is the combination of values and ethics
    being expressed through behavior.
4. A person's integrity is the presence of an internal
    government.
5. The real gauge of your actual integrity cannot be
    determined by anything other than what kind of
    person you are privately.
6. There are only two individuals that know the level
    of your integrity: you and God.
7. We should live with integrity because we have to
    live with ourselves on a daily basis.
8. We should live with integrity because other
    people are following our example.
9. We should live with integrity because we
    ultimately reap from life what we sow into it.

CONCLUSION

ECCLESIASTES 12:13–14

"Let us hear the conclusion of the whole matter: Fear God, and keep his commandments: for this is the whole duty of man. For God shall bring every work into judgment, with every secret thing, whether it be good, or whether it be evil."

This is one of my favorite texts. It really helps me to focus my life. The most significant issue surrounding this text is the condition of the writer, which is King Solomon. Solomon, at the time of writing this text, had been blessed to have a very wealthy and powerful life. He had attained what most folk waste a lifetime trying to get, and never realize. He had power, prestige, wealth, fame, and international renown. Solomon had attained all of this and discovered a very important fact of life. Through this text he allows us to peak into his mind to see his thoughts. Solomon says: "fear God and keep His commands." Solomon declares that following this is the most important undertaking of life.

Life is sometimes complex and confusing. There are many different directions that life can take us. We can become enthroned in multiple objectives. Solomon's wisdom rises from the pages of the holy writ to focus our minds on the real issue of life's purpose. Why are we here? What is our purpose?

We Are Here to Glorify God!

In 1 CORINTHIANS 6:20 Paul writes, *"For ye are bought with a price: therefore glorify God in your body, and in your spirit, which are God's."*

The greatest glory we can bring to our God is a sanctified life. If we fail to sanctify our lives to God, we will have miserably missed our real purpose for being.

One hundred years from now it will not matter how much money you made or what kind of car you drove. One hundred years from now the only thing that will remain is what you've done to please God.

The process of holiness is definitely a deeply involved effort; we are all imperfectly holy. Nonetheless, it is the heartbeat of our very existence. We live to bring glory to God. We are not perfect, but we are perfecting. We glorify Him when we resemble Him.

I pray that you continually grow into the image of our Lord. I pray that you will be accepted of Him, now and in the world to come. KEEP THE FAITH.

FOR ADDITIONAL RESOURCES OR TO
SCHEDULE THE AUTHOR FOR SPEAKING
ENGAGEMENTS, CONTACT:

R.C. BLAKES, JR. MINISTRIES
P.O. BOX 84355
PEARLAND, TX 77584

PHONE: 504-569-8205
WEBSITE: www.rcblakes.com
EMAIL: Rcblakesministries@gmail.com